Leabha.

LETTS POCKET GUIDE TO

WILD FLOWERS

The most familiar species of European
wild flowers described and illustrated in
colour

Pamela Forey and Cecilia Fitzsimons

· CHARLES LETTS ·
Letts
· FOUNDED 1796 ·

Front cover illustration: Field Poppy

This edition first published 1990
by Charles Letts & Co Ltd
Diary House, Borough Road,
London SE1 1DW

'Letts' is a registered trademark of
Charles Letts (Scotland) Ltd

This edition produced under licence by
Malcolm Saunders Publishing Ltd, London

ISBN 1 85238 103 5

Printed in Spain

Contents

Introduction

This is a book for those who want to be able to identify the wild flowers that they see on the roadsides or the "weeds" that grow in their gardens. Many people who do not have the time or opportunity to make a close study of them would still appreciate some means of easily identifying a flower that catches their eye along the roadside, in the garden, or even on waste ground or in a nature reserve.

We have selected from the several thousand European flowering plants those species most likely to be encountered in the cities, towns and villages, along the roads and tracks, and in the easily accessible countryside of Europe. The names of the plants used here are those commonly used in reference books, but you may know them under other more local names. You need not assume that you have identified a plant wrongly if you do not recognize the name, only that your name is probably one of several by which the plant is known.

How to use this book

We have divided the book into sections on the basis of flower colour, to make it as easy as possible for you to find your flower quickly.

However flowers do not always obey man-made rules. Even within a single species the flowers may range in colour from white to pink or mauve. It is also not always easy to tell exactly what colour a flower is — whether it is palest pink or white, for instance.

The book is divided into five basic sections on the basis of flower colour: **White**, **Yellow and Orange**, **Green**, **Blue and Violet**, **Red and Pink**, and **Variable**. Most of the flowers that you encounter will belong to the first five sections and you should be able to decide which section each belongs to quite easily. However, if you have a palest pink flower it might be worth while looking in both the pink and the white sections.

The last section contains flower groups like Clovers and Corydalis and plants which have variable flowers, like Comfrey. The section is quite short and it will only be necessary to use it if you have not found your flower in your original choice of colour section. It is possible that you will not be able to find your exact plant in this book for there are many wild flowers in Europe. However we have included the majority of the familiar plants as well as examples of all the major families and genera, so that you should be able to find one similar if not exactly the same.

Guide to identification

First decide to which colour section your flower belongs. You will then find that each section is further subdivided by habitat — the place where the plant is growing — indicated by the symbol at the top of the page. There are four major habitat divisions indicated by these symbols. (See Fig. 1) Many of the plants grow in one or other of these habitats, but quite a few cross the boundaries and such plants have a combination of these symbols at the top of the page.

Fig. 1 Key to habitats

Man-made habitats
Paths, tracks and roadsides; waste ground; cultivated land and fields; gardens; walls.

Open habitats
Grassland; pastures; meadows; heaths and moors; limestone and chalk downs; dunes.

Shady habitats
Hedgerows; woods and woodland edges.

Wetland habitats
Ponds and lakes; streams and ditches; watersides; marshes and fens.

The habitat classification is designed to help you confirm your identification of a flower. If you are in a dry open picnic area in open grassland, then you are only likely to find those flowering plants designated as growing in open grassland or on downs or moors. Plants designated as growing in shady woods or in wet meadows or marshes, for instance, can be eliminated.

Characteristics of your plant
Plants can rarely be identified by a single feature. It is usually the combination of flower type, flower arrangement, leaf shape and leaf arrangement that tells you that this is the right plant. The first two boxes in the description are designed to give you this information. Confirmation that this plant is found in the right habitat and in your part of Europe is given in the third box and a distribution map is provided for quick reference. Many of the plants included grow

throughout Europe. The fourth box indicates some of the similar species with which this plant might be confused.

Flowers and fruits
Information about the flowers and fruits includes the way in which the flowers grow, singly or in clusters for instance, their shape, number of petals and any peculiarities etc.; the type of fruit produced is also included, with further details if these are of particular interest in this plant. Flowering times are given at the bottom of the page but it should be noted that members of a species growing in southern Europe will come into flower earlier than members of the same species growing in northern Europe.

General form of the plant
The second box contains a more general description of the plant, its habit (whether it forms clumps or spreading mats, etc.), its leaf arrangement and leaf shape. The height of the plant is given in the box at the top of the page.

Habitat and distribution
The habitat in which a plant is found often provides an important clue to its identity, since most plants are restricted in their choice of habitat. Most of the plants included in this book grow throughout Europe, but some have more restricted distributions. The distribution is given in the Distribution Map (see Fig. 2) and more detailed information is given in the third box. It should be noted however, that the plant may not be common, or even present, throughout the whole of the area, especially if it is specialized in its habitat requirements.

Fig. 2 Distribution Map

● Commonly found in these regions
○ Present but less common or reaching the limits of its distribution

Similar and related species
In the fourth box are given some of the similar or related plants with which this one might be confused. Those similar species printed in **heavy type** are illustrated, either as featured species or in the pages of *Other Common Species*, those in ordinary type are not illustrated. Not all related or similar species have been mentioned, some of those omitted may be common in a particular locality.

Other Common Species

At the end of several of the sections you will find pages of *Other Common Species*. These are mostly less widespread than the featured plants or less likely to be encountered.

Now you are ready to use this book. It is designed to fit in your pocket, so take it with you on your next trip and don't forget to tick off your sightings on the checklist provided with the index. Remember that wild flowers are becoming ever rarer so please do not dig them up or pick them. Rare species are protected by law and it is illegal to pick the flowers in nature reserves. Photographing the flowers where they are growing provides a lasting alternative which is becoming more and more popular.

Fig. 3 Specimen Page

Colour of band denotes colour of flowers

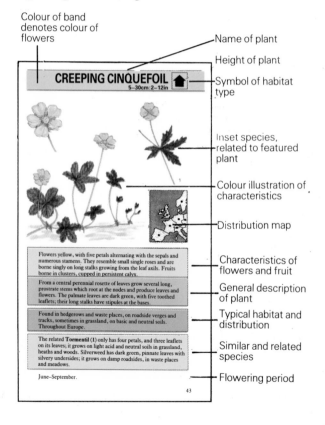

Name of plant

Height of plant

CREEPING CINQUEFOIL
5–30cm:2–12in

Symbol of habitat type

Inset species, related to featured plant

Colour illustration of characteristics

Distribution map

Flowers yellow, with five petals alternating with the sepals and numerous stamens. They resemble small single roses and are borne singly on long stalks growing from the leaf axils. Fruits borne in clusters, cupped in persistent calyx.

Characteristics of flowers and fruit

From a central perennial rosette of leaves grow several long, prostrate stems which root at the nodes and produce leaves and flowers. The palmate leaves are dark green, with five toothed leaflets; their long stalks have stipules at the bases.

General description of plant

Found in hedgerows and waste places, on roadside verges and tracks, sometimes in grassland, on basic and neutral soils. Throughout Europe.

Typical habitat and distribution

The related **Tormentil** (1) only has four petals, and three leaflets on its leaves; it grows on light acid and neutral soils in grassland, heaths and woods. Silverweed has dark green, pinnate leaves with silvery undersides; it grows on damp roadsides, in waste places and meadows.

Similar and related species

June–September.

Flowering period

43

11

Glossary

Annual A plant which grows from a seed, flowers, sets seed and dies in one year.
Biennial A plant which forms leaves in the first year, produces a flowering shoot in the second year, flowers, sets seed and dies.
Perennial A plant which lives from year to year, starting into growth again each spring.
Node A point on a stem at which the leaves are produced. On a creeping stem roots may also be produced at this point.
Succulent Crisp and juicy or soft and juicy.

Flower Structure

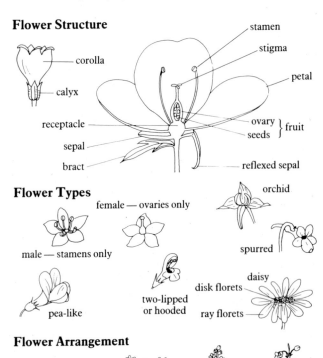

stamen
stigma
corolla
petal
calyx
receptacle
ovary
seeds } fruit
sepal
bract
reflexed sepal

Flower Types

female — ovaries only
orchid
male — stamens only
spurred
pea-like
two-lipped or hooded
daisy
disk florets
ray florets

Flower Arrangement

umbel
cluster
spike
spray

Leaf Types

simple leaves — not divided into leaflets

entire

ovate

lance-shaped

linear

toothed

lobed

sinuate

stipule — leaflike structure
at base of leafstalk

compound or divided leaves — divided into separate leaflets

palmate

clover-like

pinnate

Leaf Arrangement

alternate

opposite

rosette of
basal leaves

whorled

Fruits

Berry A juicy fruit which contains several seeds.

Capsule A dry fruit, usually rounded and containing one to several sections and many seeds. It may split open down the sides or at the top or bottom to release the seeds or it may have developed holes through which the seeds escape.

Nutlet A hard dry fruit containing a single seed. In some plant families, like the mint and borage families, the nutlets develop in groups of four.

Pod A long dry fruit, usually containing several large seeds, which splits open along one or both seams to release the seeds.

Vegetative structures

Bulb A very short underground stem with many swollen leaves growing from it, forming a foodstore for next year's plant.

Corm A swollen, underground, food-storing stem, formed at the base of the leaves and on top of last year's corm.

Offshoot A new plant formed on a short creeping stem which grows from the parent plant. Often many offshoots are formed so that the original plant may be ringed by "babies".

Runner A long creeping stem growing from a parent plant, on which new plants form at the nodes.

COMMON MOUSE-EAR CHICKWEED
15–45cm:6–18in

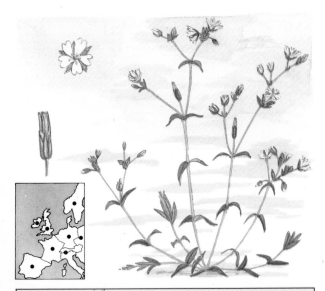

Flowers borne in loose clusters. Each has five sepals with papery margins; five white, deeply notched petals not much longer than the sepals; and ten stamens. Fruits are curved, cylindrical capsules, cupped in sepals and opening by teeth.

A small, hairy, perennial plant with creeping leafy shoots and more erect flowering stems. The leaves are dark grey-green and covered with white hairs, oblong or lance-shaped and borne in opposite pairs, sessile or with short stalks.

A weed of waste places, arable land, roadsides and tracks, grassland and coastal dunes. Found throughout Europe.

Field Mouse-ear Chickweed grows on dry banks and grassland; it has softly hairy leaves and white flowers with petals which are twice as long as the sepals. Sticky Mouse-ear Chickweed has pale yellow-green leaves and sticky, glandular shoots; it grows on walls, dunes and in waste places.

April–September.

14

1

Flowers borne in loose clusters terminating the stems. Each flower has five sepals with membranous margins; five white, deeply notched petals which are the same length as the sepals; and ten stamens. The fruiting capsules droop downwards.

An annual plant which forms small clumps of weak, leafy shoots with terminal flowers. The ovate leaves are borne in opposite pairs. There is a single line of hairs running along the stem from one node to the next.

A common weed of gardens, cultivated land, waste places and tracks throughout Europe.

Lesser Stitchwort (1) has many brittle, erect stems with linear, opposite leaves and white flowers with deeply notched petals; it grows in woods, thickets and grassland. Greater Stitchwort is similar but larger with conspicuous white flowers; it grows in woods and hedgerows.

Throughout the year.

Flowers borne in small erect spikes, individually very small with four white, spoon-shaped petals. Fruits are characteristically purse-shaped pods, like little hearts, borne on long stalks.

A small annual weed, with a rosette of basal leaves, each tapering towards the base and often deeply toothed and somewhat hairy. Leaves on flower stalk have clasping bases.

A small but distinctive weed of gardens, arable land, waste places, tracks and roadsides. Found throughout Europe.

Smith's Cress grows on arable land and roadsides; it is a small perennial plant with distinctive fruits - they are rounded with a notched wing at the top. Whitlow Grass is a small weed of walls, rocks and waste ground; it has tiny white flowers and oval fruits on long stalks.

Often throughout the year.

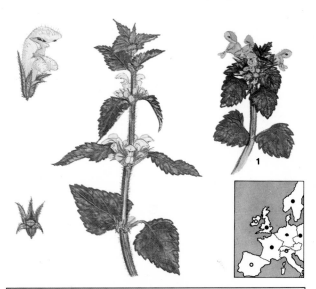

Flowers large, white and two-lipped, the upper lip hooded, the lower lip three-lobed, with a ring of hairs near the base of the tube; borne in dense whorls in upper leaf axils. Nutlets trigonal with flattened apex; produced in fours in calyces.

A perennial plant forming a clump of erect, hairy, leafy, four-angled stems. The leaves are large, long-stalked and ovate with pointed tips and toothed edges, borne in opposite pairs.

Found in waste places, hedgerows and roadsides, throughout Europe.

Red Deadnettle (1) grows in similar places but has pink-purple flowers, with purplish bracts in dense terminal spikes. Yellow Archangel has whorls of yellow flowers and serrated leaves. Henbit has rounded, scalloped leaves and pink flowers with long tubes; it grows in cultivated and waste land.

May–December.

17

White flowers have five petals; borne in umbels up to 5cm:2in across, with 5–10 flower stalks in each umbel. Outermost flowers have large outer petals. Fruits are borne in pairs, brown or black in colour, long and smooth with small beaks.

A biennial or perennial plant with a clump of ferny, divided leaves early in the year, from which grow tall leafy flowering stems. The stems are hollow with deep furrows and bear alternate, divided leaves.

Found in hedgerows, shady roadside verges, woodland edges and waste places throughout Europe.

Rough Chervil and Hedge Parsley are both hedgerow plants, the former flowering in June and July, the latter in July and August. Rough Chervil is a large, rough plant with solid, purple-spotted stems and divided leaves. Hedge Parsley's solid stems lack the purple spots; it has short-stalked umbels.

May–June.

Flowers white or pinkish; borne in large compound umbels, up to 15cm:6in across and with 10–20 stalks in each umbel. The outer flowers have large outer petals. Fruits are borne in pairs; they are round and flattened with broad wings.

A rough biennial plant with a rosette of divided leaves in the first year and a clump of erect, leafy stems in the second. The stems are hollow with well-defined hairy ridges and the large leaves have coarsely toothed, deeply lobed leaflets.

Found in hedgerows, woods and woodland edges, roadsides and grassy places throughout Europe.

Giant Hogweed is an enormous rough plant, up to 4 metres:13ft high, with a red-spotted stem; its umbels may be 60cm:24in across. It can irritate the skin. **Wild Carrot** has a central purple flower in each umbel; the umbels assume a cup shape in fruit. Hemlock has a purple-spotted stem; it is poisonous.

June–September.

GROUND ELDER
40–100cm:16–40in

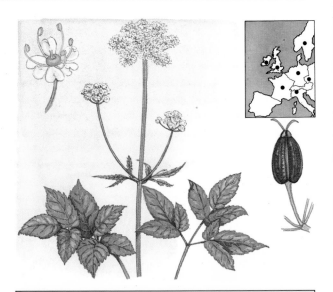

Flowers tiny with white petals, borne in compound umbels; usually umbels grow in threes, terminating the stems. The umbels have no bracts at the bases of the stalks. Fruits are borne in pairs; they are egg-shaped, flattened and ridged.

A perennial plant which spreads by creeping underground stems. From these grow dense carpets of long-stalked, divided leaves with pointed-oval, toothed leaflets. The leafy flowering stems are grooved and hollow.

A persistent weed in gardens, also grows in waste places, shady roadsides and hedgebanks in much of Europe.

Cow Parsley has ferny leaves and the outermost flowers have long outer petals. **Wild Angelica** has purplish stems and grows in marshes and fens. **Hogweed** is a larger, roughly hairy plant.

May–July.

F63539

Flowers white, with four petals; borne in small terminal clusters which lengthen somewhat as the flowers age. Fruits are long, four-angled pods borne more or less upright on short stout stalks.

A hairless, biennial plant with a rosette of long-stalked, heart-shaped leaves in the first year and an erect leafy stem with terminal flower clusters in the second. The plant smells of garlic when crushed and has been used in salads.

Found in hedgerows, woodland edges and shady places throughout Europe.

Field Penny Cress grows in waste places; it has similar white flowers but they terminate in lengthening spikes of heart-shaped, yellowish fruits. Hoary Cress is a spreading perennial weed of waste places and arable land; it has inflated heart-shaped fruits in a lengthening spike, following white flowers.

April–June.

DAISY
2–5cm:¾–2in

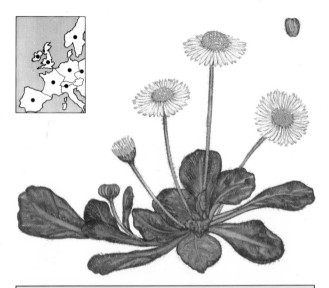

Flower heads produced singly on long stalks growing from the leaf rosettes. Each head has a central disk of yellow tube florets and an outer ring of white, often pink-tinged, ray florets. Seeds are small, oval and lack a parachute.

A small perennial plant which forms rosettes of spoon-shaped, hairy leaves close to the ground.

Found in garden lawns, on roadsides and tracks, and in short grassland throughout Europe.

Other composite plants with similar flowers are generally much larger. **Ox-eye Daisy** forms clumps of stems, up to 70cm:28in tall, with large daisy flowers. Mayweeds and chamomiles are also taller, up to 60cm:24in, with dissected leaves.

March–November.

Flower heads large and solitary, up to 5cm:2in across, with an outer circle of overlapping, long white ray florets and a central yellow disk; borne terminally on long stalks. Seeds are pale grey, ribbed and hairless.

A perennial plant with basal rosettes of long-stalked, spoon-shaped, toothed leaves. From these rosettes grow erect stalks with lobed or toothed, clasping leaves and solitary flower heads.

Found in all kinds of grassland, on roadsides and railway embankments, meadows and pastures, generally on good soils. Throughout Europe.

Chamomiles and Mayweeds have deeply lobed or lacy leaves and bear their flowers in clusters, in contrast to the Ox-eye Daisy, and some of them have strong disagreeable odours. The **Daisy** is much smaller with rosettes of spoon-shaped leaves close to the ground, and white, pink-tinged ray florets.

June-August.

SCENTLESS MAYWEED
10–60cm:4–24in

1

Flower heads are borne singly terminating the stems. Each has a ring of 12–30 outer white ray florets which droop as the flower ages, and a central flat disk of yellow tube florets. Seeds are three-ribbed, with two brown oil glands at the top.

An annual or biennial plant which forms a clump of branched, hairless stems. The stems bear many spirally arranged, dissected leaves with linear segments. In maritime forms the leaf segments may be blunt and fleshy. Scentless.

Found in waste places, cultivated and arable land, on rocks and walls, on sand and shingle by the sea. Throughout Europe.

Wild Chamomile is found in similar places but is an aromatic plant that flowers in June and July; it has a conical central disk in each flower head. **Pineapple Weed** (1) is a roadside weed which flowers in June and July; it has tall conical disks and no ray florets. **Feverfew** has a distinctive scent.

July–September.

24

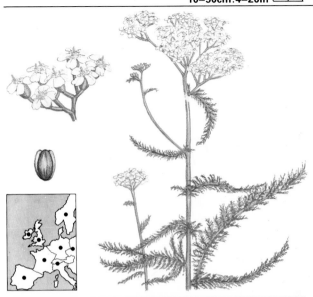

Flowers white or pink-tinged, borne in large flat, dense clusters, on top of the erect stems. Each flower head looks like a single flower but actually has five outer ray florets and a central disk of tubular florets. Seeds have small wings.

A creeping perennial plant with many woolly erect stems, bearing soft, deep green feathery leaves and terminal flower heads. The plant has a distinctive scent.

Found on roadsides and grassy banks, in grassland and meadows, and in hedgerows throughout Europe.

Yarrow is unlikely to be confused with other members of the daisy family except Sneezewort. This plant grows in damp meadows and marshes, and beside streams. It has fewer, larger flower heads in loose clusters; each has 8–13 large white ray florets and greenish white disk florets.

June–August.

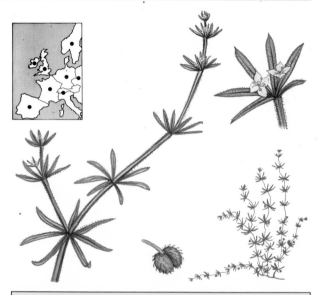

Tiny tubular flowers, with four white or greenish white petals, are borne in small clusters in the axils of the uppermost leaves. Fruits are distinctive, borne in pairs, each one small, rounded and covered in hooks.

A scrambling annual plant forming clumps of lax stems, supported by other vegetation. The four-angled stems bear hooked bristles on the angles and the linear bristly leaves are arranged in whorls of six or eight.

Found in waste places, hedgerows and woodland, on shingle beaches and hillside screes. Throughout Europe.

Hedge Bedstraw forms clumps of weakly erect stems with whorls of eight leaves. White flowers bloom in branched clusters terminating the stems, creating an effect of white froth. Woodruff is a woodland plant which forms low carpets of erect stems with whorls of leaves; it forms white flowers in spring.

June–September.

Flowers white with five deeply notched petals, their bases enclosed in a sticky tubular calyx; borne in loose, few-flowered clusters terminating stems, male and female flowers separate. Fruits are egg-shaped capsules enclosed in calyx.

A short-lived perennial plant which forms clumps of erect, rather weak, leafy stems, all covered with downy hairs. Each stem bears several pairs of opposite, elliptical leaves, the lower ones with stalks, the upper ones clasping the stem.

Found in hedgerows, waste places and cultivated ground throughout Europe.

The flowers of Bladder Campion also have white, deeply notched petals, but have distinctive bladder-like calyces. Sea Campion has similar bladder-like calyces, but is a spreading mat-forming plant which grows on shingle and cliffs near the sea. **Red Campion (1)** has rose-coloured flowers.

May–September.

WILD STRAWBERRY
5–30cm:2–12in

Flowers borne in small flat clusters on long stalks; small and white, like tiny roses, with five petals alternating with the sepals. Sepals are joined together behind the flower. Fruits are strawberries, with seeds on the surface.

A small, perennial, clump-forming plant with tufts of long-stalked, hairy leaves, each with three toothed leaflets. It forms several runners — thin, prostrate stems which root at the nodes to form new plants.

Found in open woods and woodland edges, scrub and grassland, especially on basic soils. Throughout Europe.

Garden Strawberries have much larger fruits. When in flower, Wild Strawberries may be confused with Barren Strawberries which have widely separated white petals and bluish green leaves with hairs beneath. The two are easy to distinguish in fruit for the fruits of Barren Strawberry are not fleshy.

Flowers: April–July. Fruits: June–July.

ENCHANTER'S NIGHTSHADE

20–70cm:8–28in

Flowers small, white with two sepals and two deeply bilobed petals; borne in elongated branched spikes terminating erect stems. Fruits distinctive, small green ovoids covered with pale, stiff, hooked bristles all pointing downwards.

A perennial plant which spreads by short creeping stems. The upright stems bear glandular hairs and opposite pairs of large, heart-shaped leaves, each pair growing at right angles to the pair above and below.

Found in woods and other moist, shady places on basic soils throughout Europe, where it may form extensive carpets in suitable places.

Alpine Enchanter's Nightshade grows in woods and ravines in mountain areas; it is a much smaller plant with denser spikes of flowers. A hybrid between the two species grows throughout much of Europe in shady woods and amongst rocks; it is intermediate in features between the two parents.

June–August.

WOOD SORREL
5–15cm:2–6in

Spring flowers borne singly on long stalks; they are cup-shaped and have five white petals veined with lilac. Later summer flowers are borne on short stalks close to the ground and rarely open. Fruits are rounded capsules.

A small perennial plant with creeping underground stems and tufts of leaves and flowers. Leaves grow on long stalks directly from underground stems; each has three heart-shaped yellow-green leaflets which fold down at night.

Found in woods and on shady banks, amongst damp rocks and mosses or growing on decaying logs. Throughout Europe.

Creeping Yellow Sorrel is a garden weed with prostrate, rooting stems, tufts of folding leaves and yellow flowers; some forms have purple leaves. **Clovers** have similar leaves but quite different flowers and their leaves do not fold at night.

April–August.

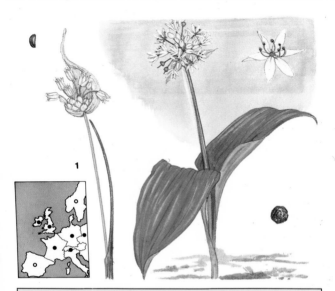

Flowers white, with six petals; borne on leafless, three-angled flower stalks in upright umbels. Papery brown membrane at base encloses buds and drops off as flowers emerge. Fruits are three-lobed with a round, pitted black seed in each lobe.

From narrow white underground bulbs grow large, bright green leaves. They have long stalks twisted through 180° and flat, pointed-elliptical blades with many parallel veins. Flowers are borne on separate stalks.

Found in damp shady places and damp woods where it may form wide colonies, scenting the air with its distinctive garlic smell. Throughout Europe.

Crow Garlic (1) has green bulbils which may replace the pink or greenish white flowers; it has hollow cylindrical leaves. Chives have leaves like those of Crow Garlic but its umbels of pink flowers lack bulbils. Triquetrous Garlic has a drooping, one-sided umbel of white flowers on a thick stem.

April–June.

31

WOOD ANEMONE
5–30cm:2–12in

Flowers solitary, white or tinged with pink; borne singly on separate stalks, high above the leaves, nodding when in bud. Each has six or seven petal-like sepals and numerous stamens. Fruits beaked, born in globular clusters on erect stems.

A perennial, carpeting plant with creeping underground stems. From these grow many erect stems which bear one or two three-lobed leaves about halfway up the stem. Poisonous and acrid.

Forms carpets of leaves and flowers in the spring and early summer in many deciduous woods throughout most of Europe. Absent from Portugal.

Yellow Wood Anemone is similar but has yellow flowers; it grows in much of Europe but is not as widespread or as common as the Wood Anemone. Blue Wood Anemone, from southeastern Europe, is also similar but has blue flowers; it is grown in gardens in northern Europe and may escape into the wild.

March–May.

Flowers white with five petals, and abundant nectar on the receptacles; they are borne in loose, branched clusters terminating the upright flowering stems, which are covered with glandular hairs. Fruits develop beneath the flowers.

A perennial plant with a basal rosette of long-stalked, rather fleshy leaves. The leaf blades are kidney-shaped with rounded lobes. The plant produces brown bulbils (small bulbs) beneath the soil, at the base of the stem.

Found in well-drained meadows and grassland, in woods and amongst rocks, on basic and neutral soils. Throughout much of Europe.

Round-leaved Saxifrage grows in shady places in mountains of continental Europe. Most other well-known saxifrages produce low-growing mats, formed of rosettes of mossy leaves or rosettes of lime-encrusted leaves. Many grow in mountainous regions.

April–June.

SNOWDROP
10–25cm:4–10in

Nodding flowers borne singly; each has three white spreading outer petals and three inner smaller green-spotted ones. Bud protected by two green membranes that dry and persist in fruit. Fruit is a green egg-shaped capsule.

From an underground bulb grows a small clump of linear grass-like leaves, blue-green in colour and emerging in spring after the flowers. Flowers grow on separate stalks. The plant dies down by summer.

Found in damp woods, meadows and beside streams. Scattered throughout much of Europe, except the north, Portugal and Ireland.

Summer Snowflake forms a 30–50cm:12–20in tall clump of bright green, linear leaves. It produces several taller, leafless flowering stalks in early summer, each with an umbel of white, green-tipped flowers.

January–March.

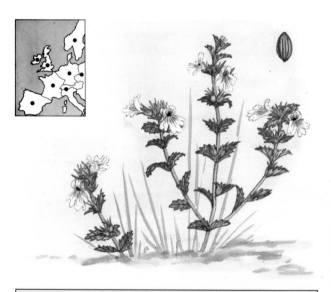

Flowers borne in terminal spike, each in the axil of a bract. They are two-lipped, upper lip has two lobes, lower lip three; white with a yellow-spotted lower lip and marked or veined with purple. Fruits are capsules, cupped in persistent calyx.

A partially parasitic, annual plant. It forms a small clump of more or less erect, branched, fine stems with spirally arranged, toothed leaves.

Found in a variety of grassy habitats, meadows, dry grassland and downs, heaths and moors, sea-cliffs and mountains, marshes and bogs. Throughout Europe.

The many species of Eyebright are difficult to distinguish from each other. However each one is restricted as to habitat and distribution and so identification can often be made on this basis. There are also small differences in leaf form and arrangement, hairiness, size and colour pattern of flowers.

June–October.

MEADOWSWEET
60–120cm:24– 48 in

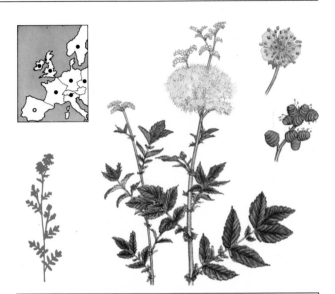

Flowers creamy white and sweet-scented; borne in dense clusters terminating the upright stems. Each has five reflexed sepals. five petals and numerous long stamens. The clusters of fruits become spirally twisted together when ripe.

A tall perennial plant with a clump of pinnate leaves and several leafy, upright stems. The leaves bear toothed, ovate leaflets in opposite pairs, larger ones alternating with smaller ones; they are dark green above, often white beneath.

Found in wet meadows, marshes, fens and wet woodland, beside streams and ditches. Throughout Europe.

Dropwort is found in dry grassland, especially on calcareous soils. It has a rosette of dark green leaves and tall, almost leafless, flower stalks bearing a dense terminal cluster of creamy white, red-tinged flowers. Each flower has six sepals and petals; they are followed by clusters of erect fruits.

June–August.

WATER PLANTAIN
20–100cm:8–40in

Flowers small and numerous, pale lilac or white with three petals; borne on erect, branched flower stalks in tiers of loose clusters, on the upper part of the stem. Seeds are flattened and borne in a whorl of about 20 on a flat disk.

A smooth, erect perennial plant with a clump of long-stalked leaves which emerge from the water. The blades of the leaves are 8–20cm:3–8in long, ovate with distinct parallel ribs. The flower stalks grow separately, directly from the base of the clump.

Found in shallow water and muddy places, in ditches, ponds, canals and slow-moving streams. Throughout Europe.

Lesser Water Plantain has linear or lance-shaped leaves, flowers produced in two whorls or in a single umbel, and fruits in rounded, crowded heads. Arrow-head produces clumps of large arrow-shaped leaves; its erect flower stalks have several whorls of three flowers. It grows in shallow water.

June–August.

SUNDEW
5–25cm : 2–10in

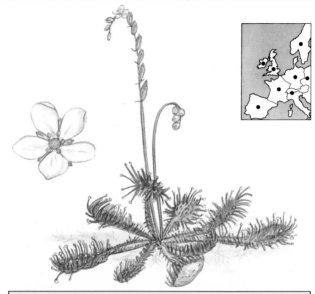

Flowers are borne on slender, arching shoots, opening one or two at a time; white or tinged with pink, with five petals. Fruits are capsules with many seeds.

A small perennial, insect-eating plant which forms little rosettes of round, long-stalked leaves. The leaves are red-green in colour, with many reddish, glistening, sticky hairs which act as insect traps.

Found in peat bogs and on wet peat on moors and heaths, often lining the edge of small pools and channels. Throughout Europe in suitable habitats.

Other Sundews are found in similar places; they differ mainly in the shape of their leaves. Great Sundew grows in the wettest areas of sphagnum bogs and has erect narrow leaves with elongated blades. Long-leaved Sundew grows in damp peat; it has erect leaves with round blades.

June–September.

38

Flowers floating, 10–20cm:4–8in across, growing on long stalks from stems buried in the mud. Each has many white, scented petals, smaller in the centre and numerous yellow stamens. Fruits are like berries, ripen under water and release floating seeds.

A perennial aquatic plant with large creeping stems buried in the mud at the bottom of the water. The round, notched leaves are borne on long stalks so that they float on the surface. They grow up to 30cm:12in across and are reddish beneath.

Found in lakes and ponds, slow-moving rivers and canals. Throughout Europe.

Yellow Water Lily has oval floating leaves and yellow floating flowers. The flowers have 5–6 large, yellow sepals forming a cup and numerous small yellow petals within. They smell of stale alcohol.

June–August.

39

OTHER COMMON SPECIES

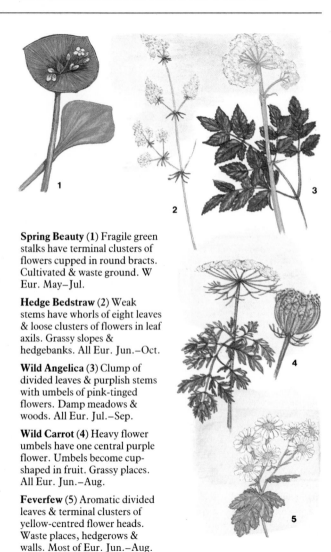

Spring Beauty (1) Fragile green stalks have terminal clusters of flowers cupped in round bracts. Cultivated & waste ground. W Eur. May–Jul.

Hedge Bedstraw (2) Weak stems have whorls of eight leaves & loose clusters of flowers in leaf axils. Grassy slopes & hedgebanks. All Eur. Jun.–Oct.

Wild Angelica (3) Clump of divided leaves & purplish stems with umbels of pink-tinged flowers. Damp meadows & woods. All Eur. Jul.–Sep.

Wild Carrot (4) Heavy flower umbels have one central purple flower. Umbels become cup-shaped in fruit. Grassy places. All Eur. Jun.–Aug.

Feverfew (5) Aromatic divided leaves & terminal clusters of yellow-centred flower heads. Waste places, hedgerows & walls. Most of Eur. Jun.–Aug.

OTHER COMMON SPECIES

Field Pansy (1) Several long stems have spoon-shaped leaves, dissected stipules & creamy flowers. Cultivated & waste land. All Eur. Mar.–Sep.

Corn Spurrey (2) Channelled stems bear whorls of linear leaves & loose flower sprays. Waste & arable land on acid soils. All Eur. Jun.–Sep.

Purging Flax (3) Slender wiry stem has small leaves & loose cluster of tiny flowers. Grassland, heaths & dunes. All Eur. Jun.–Sep.

Star of Bethlehem (4) Grassy leaves & umbels of star-like flowers. Flowers open in sun. Grassy places & cultivated land. Much of Eur. Apr.–Jun.

Black Nightshade (5) Branched stems with dull green leaves, clusters of flowers & poisonous berries. Gardens & waste places. All Eur. Jul.–Sep.

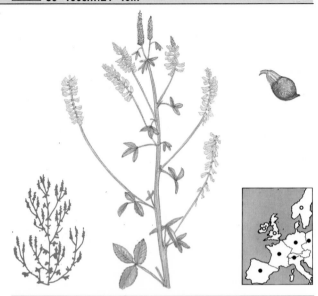

Flowers many, like yellow pea flowers, and smelling of new-mown hay; borne in loose spikes on long flower stalks in the leaf axils. Pods egg-shaped with transverse ridges and brown when ripe.

A much-branched, more or less erect biennial plant. The compound leaves each have three leaflets and a stipule clasping the base of the leaf stalk.

Found on roadsides, in fields and waste places throughout Europe.

Tall Melilot is very similar but can be recognized by its pods which are hairy and black when ripe. White Melilot has white flowers.

June–September.

42

1

Flowers yellow, with five petals alternating with the sepals and numerous stamens. They resemble small single roses and are borne singly on long stalks growing from the leaf axils. Fruits borne in clusters, cupped in persistent calyx.

From a central perennial rosette of leaves grow several long, prostrate stems which root at the nodes and produce leaves and flowers. The palmate leaves are dark green, with five toothed leaflets; their long stalks have stipules at the bases.

Found in hedgerows and waste places, on roadside verges and tracks, sometimes in grassland, on basic and neutral soils. Throughout Europe.

The related **Tormentil** (1) only has four petals, and three leaflets on its leaves; it grows on light acid and neutral soils in grassland, heaths and woods. Silverweed has dark green, pinnate leaves with silvery undersides; it grows on damp roadsides, in waste places and meadows.

June–September.

HEDGE MUSTARD
30–90cm:12–36in

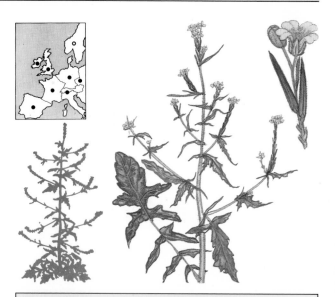

The small flowers are pale yellow with four petals. They are borne in small clusters at the tips of lengthening fruiting stems, which are held almost at right angles to the main stem. Fruits are long thin pods held close to the stem.

An annual plant which often forms a tangle of erect branches and long fruiting stems. Leaves forming the basal rosette are deeply lobed, those on main stems each has a long terminal lobe and up to three basal lobes.

Found on roadsides, waste places, arable and cultivated land throughout Europe.

One of many yellow-flowered mustards, cresses, rockets and cabbages in Europe. **Charlock** is a serious weed of arable land; it has a single erect stem, large yellow flowers, undivided toothed leaves and beaked fruits. Treacle Mustard has upright stems, with narrow toothed leaves clothing the lower parts.

May–August.

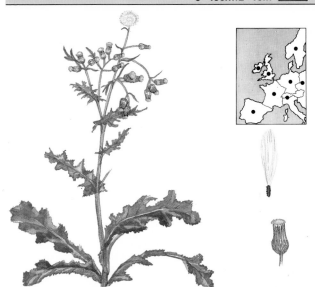

Flower heads formed only of yellow tubular florets, almost enclosed in a "cup" of green bracts; borne in small clusters in the axils of the upper leaves. The spindle-shaped seeds blow freely in the wind; they have many long white hairs.

A small annual weed with a branched leafy stem. The alternately arranged leaves are irregularly toothed and may be cottony; the upper ones have clasping bases.

A very common weed of waste places, gardens and cultivated land, roadsides and stony ground. Throughout Europe.

Stinking Groundsel grows on waste ground and tracks. It has a disagreeable odour and sticky stems; its flower heads have small inrolled ray florets. Wood Groundsel grows on sandy acid soils in open woods and heaths; it has inrolled ray florets, like Stinking Groundsel, but it is not sticky or scented.

Most of the year.

SPINY MILKTHISTLE
20–150cm : 8–60in

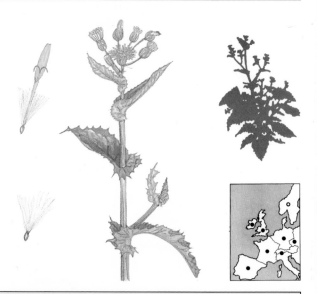

Flower heads are borne in loose umbel-like clusters terminating the branches of the stems. They have golden yellow ray florets cupped in green bracts. Seeds are flattened, brown and ribbed, with a parachute of many white hairs.

An annual plant with a clump of leaves and an erect, branched, hairless, angled stem. Stem is hollow with milky sap. Leaves are dark glossy green, variable in shape but with spiny edges. Upper leaves have ear-shaped bases which clasp the stem.

Found in waste places, on roadsides and tracks, in cultivated ground. Throughout Europe.

Common Sowthistle has dull grey-green leaves with sinuately wavy, not spiny edges; ear-like leaf bases of upper leaves do not clasp the stem. Field Milkthistle has creeping underground stems and many erect stems. The flower stalks and bracts of its flower heads are covered with glandular yellow hairs.

June–September.

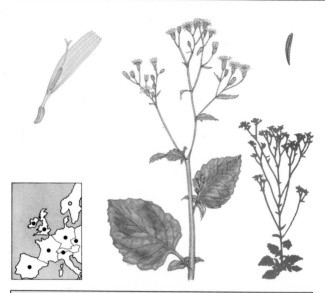

Flower heads open on bright days and close in mid afternoon;
borne in widely spreading, flat-topped clusters terminating
branches. Each has a dull yellow central disk and an outer row of
pale yellow ray florets. Seeds brown, ribbed and curved.

An annual plant with an erect stem and many upright branches on
its upper half. Lower leaves are long-stalked, with an arrow-
shaped blade and other small lobes joining the winged base.
Upper leaves smaller, usually entire, pointed and hairy.

Found in waste places, on roadsides, walls and tracks, in
hedgerows and on woodland edges. Throughout Europe.

Prickly Lettuce has prickly leaves with ear-like basal lobes; all its
leaves are held vertically in the north-south plane when it grows in
full sun. It grows in waste places and on walls. Great Lettuce
grows in grassy places and has tall stems (up to 200cm:80in),
adorned with prickly clasping leaves.

July–September.

47

Yellow flowers borne on long stalks in loose clusters in the upper leaf axils. Each has two sepals which drop as bud opens, four petals and many stamens. Fruit an elongated capsule with a row of large black seeds; each seed has a fleshy appendage.

A perennial, somewhat hairy plant forming a clump of brittle stems. Leaves deeply divided, with five to seven oval toothed leaflets, growing in a basal rosette and on the erect stems. Sap bright orange, caustic and poisonous.

Found in hedgerows, banks and at the bases of walls throughout Europe, usually close to habitation. Formerly grown as a remedy for warts.

Welsh Poppy has large solitary yellow flowers; it grows in damp shady places or amongst rocks in western Europe. **Lesser Celandine** is unrelated, is a much smaller plant and has flowers with 8–10 shiny yellow petals.

May–August.

Solitary flower heads only open in sun; borne on leafless stalks with green bracts beneath the heads. They have many golden-yellow ray florets, the outermost streaked with red beneath. Brown seeds have a single ring of feathery hairs.

A small perennial plant with a rosette of more or less hairless, lance-shaped leaves which may be sinuately toothed at edges or deeply lobed with linear divisions. Unbranched or forked flower stalks grow directly from base of rosette.

Found on roadsides and tracks, in meadows and pastures, on waste ground. Throughout Europe.

Rough Hawkbit has roughly hairy, sinuate leaves, covered with forked hairs. Its solitary flower heads have orange outer florets; its seeds have two rows of whitish hairs, an inner feathery row and an outer row of bristles. The outer florets of **Cat's Ears** are grey-green or mauve beneath.

June–October.

49

⬆◉ SMOOTH HAWKSBEARD
20—90cm:8—36in

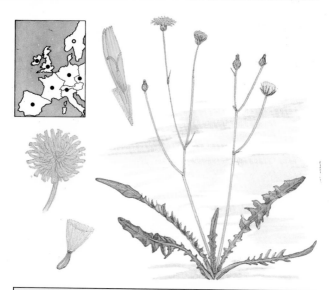

Flower heads small, up to one cm:½in across, bright yellow and often reddish beneath, cupped in two rows of greyish bracts with black bristles; borne in loose clusters on erect stems. Seeds are ribbed with many rows of soft, snow white hairs.

An annual or biennial plant with a rosette of basal leaves. These are long and narrow, irregularly toothed or lobed, more or less hairless. The branched flower stems have a few lance-shaped leaves, arrow-shaped at the base with clasping bases.

Found in grassland and pastures, on heaths, in waste places, on roadsides and walls. Throughout Europe.

There is a common variety of this plant with larger flower heads (up to 2cm:¾in in diameter) and black or blackish green bracts. Rough Hawksbeard has rough leaves without arrow-shaped bases, and larger flower heads, up to 3.5cm:1½in across. **Hawkweeds** have only one or two rows of hairs on their seeds.

June–September.

CAT'S EAR
10–60cm:4–24in

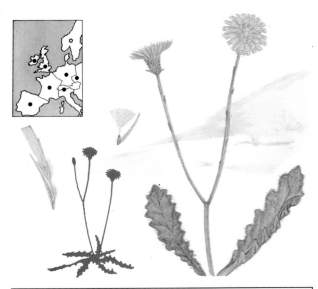

Flower heads borne on erect stems; bright yellow with many ray florets and cupped in green bracts which have hairs on the midribs. Seeds orange with a long beak, atop which is a double row of hairs, the outer row simple, the inner row feathery.

A perennial plant with a rosette of hairy, elongated leaves with sinuately wavy edges. Several flower stalks grow directly from the base of the rosette; they often fork and have many small scale-like bracts.

Found in grassy meadows, pastures and roadsides, in open woods, in garden lawns and on dunes. Throughout Europe.

Smooth Cat's Ear has small flower heads which only open in full sun; it has hairless pale green leaves. **Autumnal Hawkbit** has red streaks beneath its flower heads. **Dandelion** has hollow stems and leaves with milky sap. **Hawkweeds** have simple hairs, and **Hawksbeards** many rows of hairs, on their seeds.

June–September.

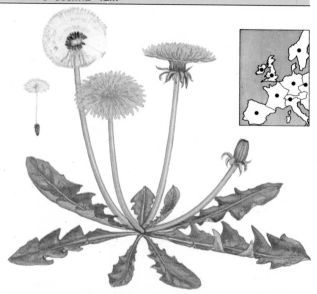

Solitary flower heads are bright yellow with ray florets only and no central disk; they are borne on hollow leafless stalks. They are followed be distinctive "clocks", round balls of seeds, each with a parachute formed of many rows of hairs.

A small rosette-forming perennial plant with a long thin taproot and a clump of deep green entire or sinuate leaves. Flower stems are hollow and they, and the leaves, exude white "milk" when broken, which stains the fingers.

A familiar weed of lawns and gardens, roadsides and tracks, waste ground and other grassy places throughout Europe.

Other similar plants, like **Cat's Ears** and **Hawkbits** have solid stems without milky juice. **Hawkweeds** and **Hawksbeards** have solid, leafy flower stems, usually branched with many flower heads.

Mainly March–June.

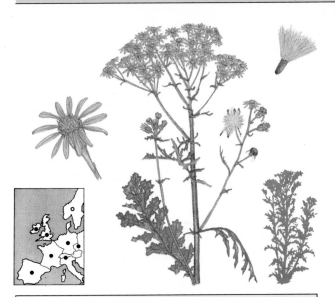

Flower heads are borne in dense clusters terminating the stem branches; each has 12–15 yellow ray florets and a central yellow disk. Seeds are dark grey-brown with a parachute of simple whitish hairs which often fall off.

A biennial or perennial plant which forms a rosette of leaves which soon die off, and a clump of branched, erect, leafy furrowed, cottony stems. Leaves are deeply divided, dark green above, white cottony beneath, upper leaves clasping the stem.

A weed of waste land, roadsides, neglected fields and grassland; also common on dunes near the sea. Throughout Europe.

Hoary Ragwort has creeping underground stems. It grows most often on grassy slopes on heavy soils. Marsh Ragwort grows in marshes, ditches and wet meadows; it has fewer larger flower heads. Oxford Ragwort is an annual sprawling, hairless plant, native to southern Europe and introduced in Britain.

June–October.

53

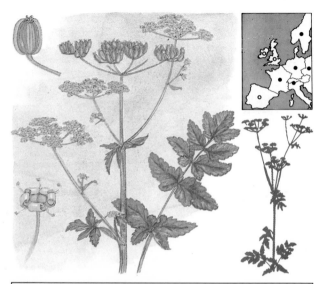

Flowers borne in compound umbels, 3–10cm:1¼–4in across, growing on long stalks in upper leaf axils. Flowers are tiny with five inrolled yellow petals. Fruits are borne in pairs; they are oval and flattened with narrow wings.

A biennial, strongly scented plant with a rosette of divided ferny leaves in the first year. In the second year an erect, hollow, furrowed stem is produced, bearing alternate ferny leaves and umbels of flowers.

Found on roadsides, in grassy places and beside tracks throughout Europe, especially on chalk and limestone.

Fennel has feathery leaves, yellow flowers and a distinctive scent. It grows on waste ground and tracksides, being native to southern Europe and naturalized further north. Alexanders has dark green leaves with rhomboidal leaflets, yellow flowers and a celery-like scent; it grows in waste places by the sea.

July–September.

BUTTERCUPS
15–100cm:6–40in

Flowers bowl-shaped, with five bright yellow, overlapping petals, shiny on the inside; borne on long, upright, branching stalks. Followed by clusters of green beaked fruits, each fruit containing a single seed.

Perennial plants, with basal rosettes of long-stalked, deeply divided leaves. From these grow erect, branched stems bearing a few similar leaves and flowers on long stems in the leaf axils. All have acrid sap.

Found in grassland and meadows, often in damp places or on heavy soils. **Creeping Buttercup** (2) grows as a weed in lawns and gardens. Throughout Europe.

Meadow Buttercup (1) forms clumps of branched stems growing from rosettes of leaves. Creeping Buttercup (2) has many runners which root at the nodes and form new rosettes. Bulbous Buttercup is found in dry grassland; its sepals are reflexed and it produces a tuberous swelling at the base of the stem.

May–August.

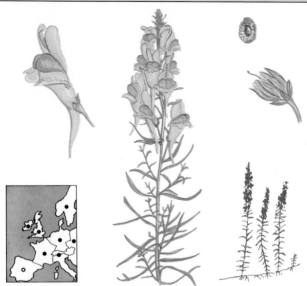

Flowers like snapdragons, bright yellow with orange palates and long straight spurs; borne in dense leafy spikes at tops of stems. Fruits are five-lobed capsules cupped in persistent calyx. Seeds are flattened with a broad wing all round.

A perennial plant with creeping underground stems, from which spring many erect, hairless flowering stems, clothed with linear, bright green leaves.

Found in hedgebanks and on roadsides, in grassland and on cultivated ground throughout Europe.

Pale Toadflax has white or pale purple flowers with conspicuous purple veins and an orange spot on the palate. It grows in dry stony places and waste ground.

July–October.

Flowers yellow with five petals, crowded together and opening a few at a time on the very tall, erect, woolly flower spike. Fruits are woolly capsules.

A biennial plant with a rosette of large woolly leaves in the first year and a tall flowering stem in the second. The bases of the leaves run down the stem funnelling water to the roots. Woolly texture of the leaves is due to many star-shaped hairs.

Found on roadsides, in waste places and on sunny banks, especially on dry soils. Throughout Europe.

White Mullein has leaves which are dark green above, covered with white hairs beneath; it has spikes of small white or yellow flowers. Dark Mullein has dark green leaves and spikes of yellow, purple-spotted flowers.

July–September.

Shiny yellow flowers are borne single on long fleshy stalks. Each has three sepals, eight to ten petals which fade to white as they age, and numerous stamens. Clusters of green beaked fruits each contain a single seed, but often they do not set.

A small, hairless, perennial plant which spreads rapidly by means of underground root tubers, so that it makes wide green carpets. Individual plants have rosettes of long-stalked, heart-shaped, glossy dark green leaves. Poisonous and acrid.

Appears in spring and early summer in woods, shady banks and hedgerows, on stream banks and in meadows throughout Europe. Dies down in summer.

Buttercups have divided, not heart-shaped leaves, fewer petals and five sepals. **Greater Celandine** is larger and is related to poppies; it is hairy, with divided leaves and its flowers have four petals.

March–May.

PRIMROSE

10–20cm:4–8in

Flowers borne singly on long stalks growing directly from the rosette. They are pale yellow with deeper yellow centres, tubular in shape, with five spreading petal-lobes above a cylindrical, hairy calyx. Fruits are round capsules.

A short-lived perennial plant with a rosette of large, wrinkled, rather spoon-shaped leaves; the leaves are deep green above, pale and hairy beneath, gradually narrowing towards the base and with green-winged stalks.

Found in hedgerows and woods, meadows and damp grassland in shady places throughout Europe.

Cowslips grow in grassland on alkaline soils. Their scented flowers are borne in umbels on long drooping stalks. They are deep yellow with orange spots. Oxlips are less common woodland plants; their flowers are like those of Cowslips but unscented and borne in one-sided clusters.

March–May.

1

Flower heads solitary, or borne in a terminal, flat-topped cluster or on long stems in the leaf axils; formed of bright yellow ray florets. Seeds cylindrical in shape, with one or two rows of simple whitish or pale brown hairs.

Perennial plants, some with rosettes of leaves, others with leaves spirally arranged on the flowering stem. Leaves simple, often lance-shaped, toothed or with wavy margins, often hairy.

Found in woods, amongst shady rocks or beside walls and banks, on heaths or in grassy places. Many grow in mountain areas. Throughout Europe.

The many hawkweeds in Europe are difficult to distinguish from each other. **Mouse-ear Hawkweed (1)** is different, for its pale yellow flowers are streaked with red beneath and it reproduces by runners. **Hawksbeards** have many rows of hairs on the seeds. Seed hairs of **Cat's Ears** and **Hawkbits** are feathery.

June–October.

60

COMMON ST JOHNS WORT

30–90cm:12–36in

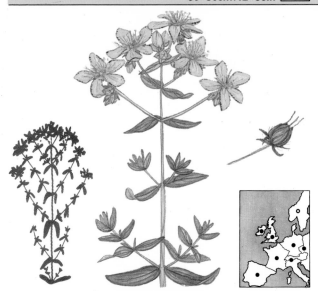

Flowers numerous, borne in branched clusters at the tops of the stems. Each has five yellow petals with black dots on the margins and, like other St John's Worts, many yellow stamens at the centre.

A hairless, branched perennial plant, spreading by leafy offshoots. The stems bear many opposite, stalkless ovate leaves, marked with translucent dots.

Found in grassland, open woodland, grassy banks and hedgerows throughout Europe.

One of many St John's Worts. Hairy St John's Wort has downy oval leaves and pale yellow flowers; it grows in hedges and shady places. Slender St John's Wort grows in woods and grassy places on acid soils; it has red-tinged petals. Imperforate St John's Wort lacks translucent spots on its leaves.

June–September.

The numerous bright yellow flowers are borne in many dense whorls terminating the main branches. Individual flowers are tiny, funnel-shaped with four pointed petal lobes. Tiny fruits are smooth and hairless, green at first, later turning black.

A perennial plant with a clump of branched, weakly erect, four-angled, sparsely hairy stems. These bear whorls of eight to twelve needle-like leaves, dark green above, paler beneath. The plant turns black when dried and smells of new-mown hay.

Found in grassy places and meadows, hedgebanks and roadsides, and on stable sand dunes. Throughout Europe.

Crosswort grows in woods and hedgerows. It has weakly erect stems with pointed-elliptical leaves in whorls of four, all covered in long, bristly white hairs. Whorls of pale yellow flowers grow in clusters in the axils of the leaves.

June–September.

BIRD'S-FOOT TREFOIL
10—40cm:4—16in

Pea-like flowers yellow or streaked with red; borne in clusters of
up to eight flowers on long stalks in the leaf axils. The cluster of
pods which follows resembles a bird's foot. Pods twist as they
open.

A small, mat-forming, somewhat hairy, perennial plant with
many thin branching stems clothed with compound leaves. The
stems are more or less solid. Each leaf has five leaflets, two of
which are situated at the base of the leaf stalk.

Found in dry grassy places, downs and meadows, in fields and on
roadsides. Throughout Europe.

Large Bird's-foot Trefoil is found in damp grassy places; it has
upright, hollow stems and spreads by underground stems. Many
small mat-forming plants with yellow flowers are found in the pea
family, including Medicks and Hop Trefoils but their flowers are
usually smaller and often borne in distinct heads.

June–August.

BITING STONECROP
2–10cm:¾–4in

Flowers borne in terminal clusters at the tops of flowering stems. They are like yellow stars, with five pointed petals and are followed by brown star-like fruits.

A mat-forming perennial plant with prostrate stems, from which grow short erect, leafy stems and tall, leafy flower-bearing stems. Leaves are dark green, stalkless and overlapping, blunt and fleshy. They are hot and biting to the taste.

Found on walls, rocks and dry grassland, especially on calcareous soils, dunes and shingle throughout Europe.

Rock Stonecrop is similar but has taller flowering stems and seven petals in the flowers. It is less widely distributed in the wild but often grown in rock gardens and naturalized. White Stonecrop is larger with white star-like flowers borne in terminal clusters; it grows on walls, rocks and roofs.

June–July.

Erect stems, produced before the leaves, are clothed with purple or green linear scale leaves; they grow up to 15cm:6in tall and each bears a terminal flower head with a yellow disk and many yellow ray florets. Pale seeds have whitish hairs.

A perennial plant with scaly white underground stems and rosettes of leaves. The leaves are long-stalked, with large, pointed heart-shaped, shallowly lobed blades, up to 30cm:12in across with branched veins. Young leaves are white-felted.

Found in waste places, on roadsides and banks, as a weed in disturbed and cultivated ground; also on streamsides, shingle banks beside streams, screes and dunes. Throughout Europe.

No other plant resembles this when it is in flower. Butterbur grows in damp meadows and on streamsides. It is a large plant, with leaves like those of Coltsfoot but up to 90cm:36in across. Its flower heads appear before the leaves; the flower stalks grow up to 40cm:16in high and bear ovoid clusters of mauve flower heads.

February–April.

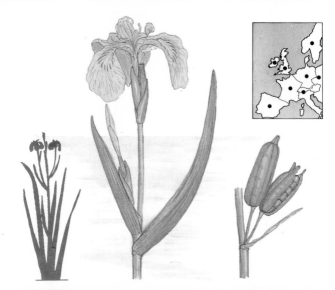

Flowers are large and bright yellow, with three outer reflexed petals often veined with purple, and three inner erect petals. They grow in clusters on tall flower stalks, cupped in green bracts. Fruits are elliptical green capsules with brown seeds.

A perennial plant with a thick underground stem from which grow clumps of erect, sword-like leaves. Branched flower stalks grow separately; they are often taller than the leaves and somewhat flattened.

Found in shallow water at the margins of ponds, canals and ditches, in marshes and wet woodland. Throughout Europe.

Stinking Iris grows in woods and hedges or on cliffs near the sea. Its leaves have a disagreeable odour when bruised. Its dull purple flowers are streaked with yellow and followed by capsules with bright red seeds. The seeds remain attached to the capsules after they have split open.

May–July.

Marsh Marigold (1) Clump of long-stalked, heart-shaped, hairless leaves with flowers in spring. Wet meadows, woods, beside streams. All Eur.

Monkeyflower (2) Creeping stems & erect leafy stems with tubular, two-lipped flowers. Banks of streams, marshes. Much of Eur. Jun.–Sep.

Bog Asphodel (3) Flowers have six petals & orange-tipped woolly stamens. Leaves grass-like. Wet acid heaths & moors, bogs. W Eur. Jul.–Aug.

Silverweed (4) Mats of silvery pinnate leaves with toothed leaflets. Flowers solitary, in leaf axils. Damp grassy places. All Eur. Jun.–Aug.

Yellow Loosestrife (5) Tall clump of leafy stems with whorls of flowers in upper leaf axils. Marshes, river & pond banks. All Eur. Jun.–Aug.

67

OTHER COMMON SPECIES

Common Rockrose (1)
Straggling mat-forming plant
with thin stems & opposite
leaves. Downs & limestone
grassland. All Eur. Flowers
May–Aug.

Lesser Yellow Trefoil (2) Small
with slender stems & clover-like
leaves. Tiny heads of flowers in
leaf axils, Jun.–Sep. Grassy
places. All Eur.

Wood Avens (3) Straggling
clump of long-stalked, three-
lobed leaves. Flower clusters
followed by hooked fruits. Most
of Eur. May–Sep.

Common Agrimony (4) Erect
stem with toothed, pinnate
leaves & spike of small flowers,
followed by conical, spiny fruits.
All Eur. Jun.–Sep.

Lady's Mantle (5) Clumps of
soft, rounded-lobed, hairy
leaves. Spray of flowers on long
stalks, May–Sep. Woods &
meadows. All Eur.

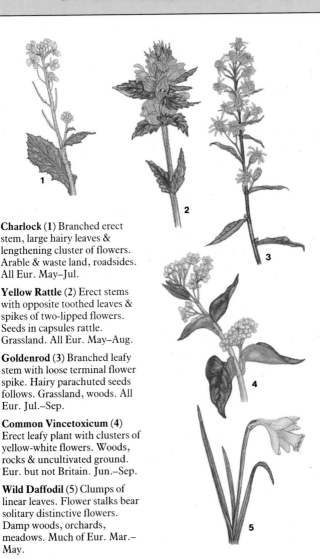

Charlock (1) Branched erect
stem, large hairy leaves &
lengthening cluster of flowers.
Arable & waste land, roadsides.
All Eur. May–Jul.

Yellow Rattle (2) Erect stems
with opposite toothed leaves &
spikes of two-lipped flowers.
Seeds in capsules rattle.
Grassland. All Eur. May–Aug.

Goldenrod (3) Branched leafy
stem with loose terminal flower
spike. Hairy parachuted seeds
follows. Grassland, woods. All
Eur. Jul.–Sep.

Common Vincetoxicum (4)
Erect leafy plant with clusters of
yellow-white flowers. Woods,
rocks & uncultivated ground.
Eur. but not Britain. Jun.–Sep.

Wild Daffodil (5) Clumps of
linear leaves. Flower stalks bear
solitary distinctive flowers.
Damp woods, orchards,
meadows. Much of Eur. Mar.–
May.

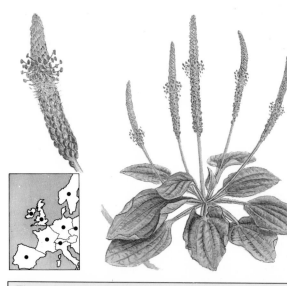

Flowers borne in spikes usually about 30cm:12in long, appearing to be green since the whitish petals are so small. Anthers conspicuous, at first mauve, later yellowish. Fruiting spike similar in shape, but brown with many small, hard fruits.

A perennial rosette-forming plant with many broad, rounded, almost hairless, long-stalked leaves, each up to 20cm:8in long. These leaves have well defined veins.

Found in open places, on roadsides and waste ground, paths and tracks and in cultivated land, farmyards and gardens. Throughout Europe.

Hoary Plantain grows in grassland; it has similar leaves to Great Plantain but short flower spikes with purplish stamens. Another very common species is Ribwort. This has long, narrow, upright leaves, and long stems with short fat flower spikes and conspicuous white anthers.

May–October.

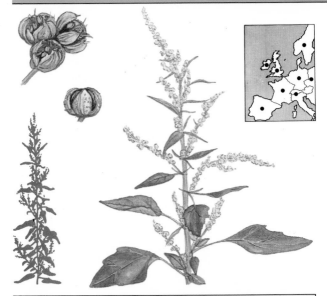

Flowers small and green with five green petals, borne in dense leafy spikes made up of many smaller flower clusters. Seeds brown and enclosed in persistent petals.

A large annual weed with reddish, mealy stems (covered with bladder-like hairs) and large leaves. Leaves toothed lowermost broad and rhomboidal, uppermost lance-shaped, deep green above and mealy beneath.

Found in farm yards, waste places, on roadsides and cultivated ground, particularly where soil is rich in nitrogen. Throughout Europe.

Good King Henry is a very similar perennial plant of farmyards and roadsides; it has triangular leaves which are mealy when young. Other related less common goosefoots are found near the sea, on waste land and several alien N. American species may be found near docks and rubbish tips.

July–October.

Male and female flowers separate; they are tiny and green, borne in cups with long-horned half-moon shaped glands on the rims. Flowers grow in loose umbels, cupped in leafy bracts. Fruits are ridged capsules, each with three sections.

An annual plant with an erect branched stem, smooth, hairless and leafy. The leaves are soft, bright green, ovate in shape with short stalks, arranged alternately low on the stem, in opposite pairs higher up. The stems have poisonous milky sap.

Found on roadsides and waste places, and as weeds in gardens, cultivated and arable land. Throughout Europe.

There are many spurges in Europe, some of them common. Many like Petty Spurge and **Sun Spurge** (1) are annual weeds with a single branched shoot and terminal umbels of typical green spurge flowers. Others, like Wood Spurge, are perennial spreading plants with many leafy shoots.

April–November.

Flowers borne singly, on erect stalks growing from leaf axils. Each has four oval, hooded, green sepals and four minute white petals. The flower stalks droop when flowering is over, becoming erect again when the fruiting capsules ripen.

A small, prostrate, bright green, perennial plant with a dense central rosette from which grow long, fine, rooting stems. These stems are clothed with tiny, linear, opposite leaves and become erect during flowering.

A small weed of gardens, lawns, paths, grassy verges and roadsides; also grows on the banks of streams. Found throughout Europe.

Other Pearlworts include Common Pearlwort, an annual plant which has a loose central rosette and more or less erect flowering stems; and Knotted Pearlwort which forms tufts of stems with clusters of tiny leaves in the upper leaf axils, giving it a knotted appearance; it is found in damp places.

May–September.

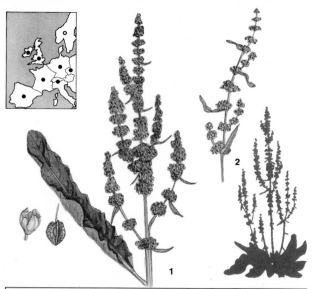

Flowers greenish brown in colour and borne in whorls on large, upright, branching spikes. Fruits are more colourful than flowers, three-sided in shape, often with three unequal red swellings in the angles.

Large perennial weeds, with a long tap root and a clump of large, long-stalked leaves, varying in their shape and in their edges depending on species. A traditional remedy for nettle stings.

Found in waste places, on cultivated ground and in gardens where they may be serious weeds, in grassland, on shingle beaches and dunes. Throughout Europe.

Common species include **Curled Dock (1)** with long leaves with distinctive curly edges; Broad-leaved Dock with wavy, not curly edges to the leaves; and **Sharp Dock (2)** with flowers borne in widely separated whorls within the flower spike. Sheep's Sorrel and **Sorrel** are common weeds of heaths and grassland.

Summer, followed by fruits in autumn.

Flowers small and petalless; borne in green "tassels" in the axils of the leaves, male and female flowers on separate plants. Fruits are small seed-like nutlets enclosed in the persistent calyx.

A large perennial plant, with a clump of upright, four-angled stems, bearing pairs of roughly toothed, deep green, pointed leaves. The whole plant is clothed with stinging hairs.

Found in waste places and on cultivated land, beside tracks and roads, in woods and hedges. Throughout Europe.

The similar Small Nettle is less common; it is an annual plant which grows up to 30cm:12in tall. It has deeply toothed leaves and male and female flowers are borne together on the same plant. Nettles may be mistaken for **Deadnettles** which have no stinging hairs but have large hooded flowers.

June–August.

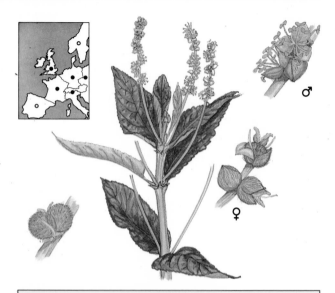

Flowers are green, petalless and inconspicuous, with male and female flowers on separate plants. They are borne on long stalks in upper leaf axils, male flowers in clusters, female singly or in twos or threes. Fruits hairy, in two sections.

A hairy perennial plant with creeping underground stems from which grow erect, leafy unbranched stems. The leaves are elliptical and pointed, dark green and toothed, borne in opposite pairs. **Very poisonous**, with a foetid scent.

Found in woods and other shady places, amongst rocks on good soils, often forming extensive carpets on the ground. Throughout Europe.

Annual Mercury grows on waste ground or as a weed; it is an annual hairless plant. It has male and female flowers on separate plants, female flowers in stalkless clusters in the leaf axils, male flowers on long stalks.

February–May.

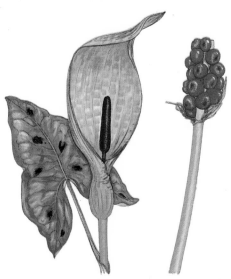

The flower is a long dull purple spike hooded by a pale green, spotted spathe. The base of this encloses the male stamens and female ovaries. The ovaries enlarge into a spike of **poisonous** red berries by late summer; the spathe meanwhile shrivels up.

A perennial plant which forms a clump of large, long-stalked, arrow-shaped leaves and a flowering spike each spring. Leaves are often spotted with dark spots, smooth, shiny and hairless. Sap is acrid and irritant.

Found in hedgerows and banks, in woods and other shady places, especially on calcareous soils. In much of Europe to southern Sweden, rare in Scotland and absent from northern Europe.

Italian Arum has a yellow spike and a pale yellow spathe. Its leaves appear in autumn and winter, the early leaves often being white-veined. This plant is native to southern and western Europe but is often grown in gardens elsewhere.

April–May. Berries: July–August.

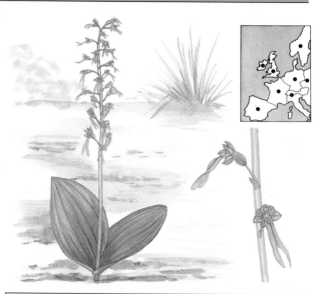

Flowers green, with a long, forked, yellow-green lower lip hanging down. The centre of this lip glistens with nectar. The flowers grow on short stalks on a long, loose spike at the top of the flowering stem. Fruits are globular capsules.

A perennial plant with a thick hairy underground stem. It produces leaves in opposite pairs in spring. The leaves are broadly ovate with pointed tips and three to five prominent ribs. The flowering stem grows up between the leaves.

Found in woods, in scrub and meadows, usually in damp places; also in damp shady lanes. It is more common on basic soils. Throughout Europe.

Lady's Tresses have white flowers in a spirally twisted flower spike; they grow in damp grassland and pastures. Broad Helleborine has leafy flower stalks with spirally arranged pointed-ovate leaves and green or dull purple flowers. These have a purplish hood and a heart-shaped, scoop-like lower lip.

May–July.

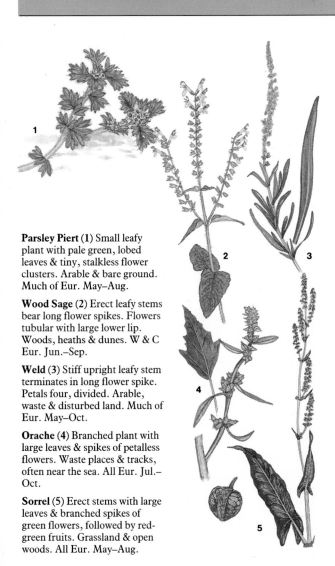

Parsley Piert (1) Small leafy plant with pale green, lobed leaves & tiny, stalkless flower clusters. Arable & bare ground. Much of Eur. May–Aug.

Wood Sage (2) Erect leafy stems bear long flower spikes. Flowers tubular with large lower lip. Woods, heaths & dunes. W & C Eur. Jun.–Sep.

Weld (3) Stiff upright leafy stem terminates in long flower spike. Petals four, divided. Arable, waste & disturbed land. Much of Eur. May–Oct.

Orache (4) Branched plant with large leaves & spikes of petalless flowers. Waste places & tracks, often near the sea. All Eur. Jul.–Oct.

Sorrel (5) Erect stems with large leaves & branched spikes of green flowers, followed by red-green fruits. Grassland & open woods. All Eur. May–Aug.

Flower heads are borne in small clusters in axils of the uppermost leaves; each has many bright blue ray florets. Flowers open in the early morning and close soon after noon. Seeds are pale brown with a ring of scales at the top.

A perennial plant forming an erect clump of tough, grooved, branched stems, often roughly hairy. Leaves spirally arranged; lower leaves are long with wavy, toothed edges, upper leaves are simpler and smaller, and may have clasping bases.

Found on roadsides and in waste places, in fields and uncultivated ground. Throughout Europe.

Endive may become naturalized in southern Europe; it is an annual with swollen stems beneath the clusters of flower heads. Cornflowers grow in waste places and cornfields. They are annuals with greyish leaves; their flower heads have bright blue marginal florets and red-purple central florets.

June–October.

Flowers bright blue with five petals and a yellow ring in the centre; calyx tubular with hooked hairs. Flowers borne in one-sided, coiled clusters which lengthen and straighten as fruits form. Fruits dark brown, shining nutlets enclosed in calyx.

An annual or biennial plant which forms a small rosette of soft, hairy, ovate leaves, and several weak flower stalks. These bear alternate, oblong or lance-shaped, stalkless leaves covered with spreading hairs.

Found on roadsides, in woodland, cultivated ground and on dunes. Throughout Europe.

There are many species of forget-me-not in Europe. Several Water Forget-me-nots grow beside streams and ponds, in marshes and wet places on mountains. Yellow-and-blue Forget-me-not has tiny flowers which open yellow and white, later turning blue.

April–July.

Flowers borne in few-flowered whorls in upper leaf axils of ascending stems. Each is violet in colour, tubular and two-lipped with purple spots on the lower lip and hairy inside the tube. Fruits are smooth nutlets, produced in fours in calyces.

A perennial plant with long, creeping stems rooting at the nodes. It has many opposite pairs of hairy, kidney-shaped leaves which may turn red at the edges in sunny positions. Creeping stems turn upwards at the ends to produce flowers.

Found in waste places, hedgerows, woods and grassland especially on damp, heavy soils. Throughout Europe.

Deadnettles have pointed-ovate leaves. **Bugle** has smooth crinkled leaves with wavy edges; it makes rosettes of leaves wherever its creeping stems take root.

March–May.

82

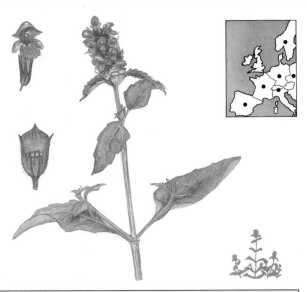

The purplish blue flowers are two-lipped, the upper lip hooded and the lower lip three-lobed; they have hairy, purplish calyces. They are borne in dense terminal spikes with hairy, purple-tinged bracts. Fruit consists of four ridged nutlets.

A small, hairy, perennial plant, forming a clump of four-angled, leafy stems that lie on the ground and then turn upwards to bear flower spikes. The deep green, opposite leaves are simple and ovate.

Found on roadsides and in lawns, in waste places, grassland and open woodland throughout Europe.

Cut-leaved Selfheal is found in much of Europe except the north; it has deeply cut, linear leaves. Large Selfheal is also widespread but absent from the west and north; its flowers are 2–2.5cm:¾–1in long, about twice the size of the flowers of Selfheal.

June–September.

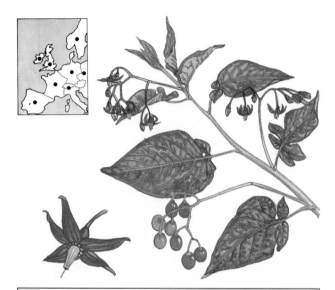

Flowers have five purple petals forming tube, with petal-lobes first spreading then reflexed, and five protruding yellow anthers; borne in drooping clusters on stalks opposite leaves. Poisonous berries are green at first, turning yellow then red.

A scrambling woody, perennial plant with alternate leaves. The leaves are long-stalked, with a large pointed-oval or arrow-shaped blade and often other smaller lobes at the base.

Found in waste ground, hedgerows and woods, on fences, dunes and shingle beaches near the sea. Throughout Europe.

Black Nightshade is a weed of gardens and waste places. It has dull, dark green, triangular leaves and clusters of white flowers followed by black berries. Yellow Nightshade has softly hairy, gray leaves and yellow fruits; it is found in much of Europe but not in the west or north.

June–September.

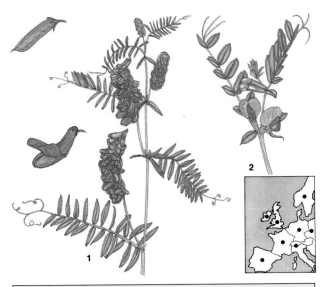

Flowers pea-like but with the wings attached to the keel, usually blue or purple in colour; borne singly, in small clusters or on long sprays in the leaf axils. Pods flattened from side to side, opening by two valves.

Annual to perennial twining plants, with thin vine-like stems and tendrils on the leaves. Leaves alternate, pinnate, usually with 6–20 opposite leaflets and with the simple or branched tendril at the end.

Found in grassy places and hedgerows, woods, thickets and bushy places throughout Europe.

Several of the vetches are widespread and common. **Tufted Vetch** (**1**) has many blue flowers in one-sided sprays. The purple flowers of **Common Vetch** (**2**) grow singly or in pairs. Bush Vetch has short-stalked clusters of up to six flowers. Wood Vetch has white flowers with blue veins, borne in long sprays.

May–September.

Flowers usually blue, borne singly, in terminal sprays or in sprays in the leaf axils. Each flower is tubular with four petal-lobes, the top lobe larger than the other three. Fruits are capsules cupped in persistent sepals.

Erect or prostrate, annual or perennial plants, forming a dense mat or clump of stems with opposite, simple, often toothed leaves. These may be hairless or covered with fine hairs. Many are weeds while some are garden species.

Found in lawns and gardens, hedges, waste and cultivated ground, woods, heaths and grassland. Some are wetland species of streams and marshes. Throughout Europe.

Germander (1) and **Common** (2) **Speedwells** are common as garden weeds, in woods and grassland. Thyme-leaved Speedwell has solitary, pale blue flowers; it grows on heaths and in grassland, as does the blue-flowered Wall Speedwell. Water Speedwell and Brooklime grow in ponds and streams.

March–September.

Spring flowers are distinctive with five blue-violet petals and a whitish spur at the back; they are unscented. They are borne on long stalks growing from the leaf axils. Later flowers do not open but produce fruiting capsules.

A perennial plant which forms a small clump of long-stalked leaves, together with slender stems which bear both leaves and flowers. The leaves resemble rounded hearts and have fringed stipules at the bases of their stalks.

Found in woodland, hedgerows, pastures and heaths throughout Europe, often in shady but not in very wet conditions.

Sweet Violets grow in hedgebanks and scrub on alkaline soils. They are similar to Dog Violets but have prostrate, rooting stems and their flowers are sweetly scented. Heath Violets grow on heaths and dry grassland; they have many, more or less prostrate stems, with heart-shaped leaves and blue flowers.

April–June.

Flowers blue, two-lipped with a ring of hairs inside, a very short upper lip and a three-lobed lower lip. Stamens protrude from the tube. Calyx bell-shaped and hairy, with five teeth; it persists to enclose the four brown, reticulate nutlets.

A perennial mat-forming plant with long, leafy runners which form a series of leaf rosettes at the nodes. Leaves smooth, hairless, and crinkled, long-stalked, ovate with wavy margins. Flower stalks with opposite leaves grow from the rosettes.

Found in damp places, in woods and meadows throughout Europe.

Skullcap grows beside water and in damp meadows. It has erect, branched stems with pairs of toothed, lance-shaped leaves and pairs of blue-violet flowers in leaf axils. Black Horehound is a hedgerow plant with a foetid smell; it forms branched stems with whorls of purple, white-marked flowers in leaf axils.

May–July.

LESSER PERIWINKLE
30–60cm:12–24in

Flowers are bright blue, borne singly on long stalks in the axils of the leaves. Each is tubular with five, spreading petal-lobes and a white ring at the centre. Fruits consist of two long pods from each flower.

A trailing, shrubby, evergreen plant with thin creeping stems which root at the nodes. From these rooted nodes grow short, upright, leafy stems. The leaves are elliptical with pointed tips, hairless and borne on short stalks in opposite pairs.

Found in hedgebanks, woods and amongst rocks in much of Europe but absent from the north.

Greater Periwinkle grows up to 100cm:40in high. Its stems are thin and flexible and root at the tips if they touch the ground. The leaves are oval with pointed tips or heart-shaped. Bright blue flowers grow in small clusters in the axils of the uppermost leaves.

March–May.

89

BLUEBELL
20–50cm:8–20in

Bright blue cylindrical flowers have three similar petals and sepals, joined at base; borne on long, naked stalks in one-sided clusters, erect in bud, drooping as they open. Capsules split into three sections when ripe, releasing black seeds.

Forms wide carpets of sappy, linear, grass-like leaves in spring, growing from underground bulbs. The leaves die down in summer. Flowers are borne on separate stalks.

Found in woods, hedgerows, banks or in grassland near the sea. Western Europe from Britain, through Belgium, France into Iberia. Introduced into northern Germany and northern Italy.

Spanish Bluebell has broader leaves and conical clusters of erect, bell-shaped, pale blue flowers; it is native to southern Europe but is grown in gardens in northern Europe and may escape. **Harebell** is a small unrelated plant; it has heart-shaped leaves and bell-shaped flowers with five petal-lobes.

April–May.

Blue-lilac flowers are borne on long stalks, in a few dense, flat, circular, terminal heads, up to 4cm:1½in across. Each head contains up to 50 flowers; the outer flowers have much longer petals than the inner ones. Fruits are dark brown and hairy.

A perennial, grey-green plant covered with stiff, downwardly pointing hairs. It has an overwintering rosette of simple leaves and one or two erect stems in summer. These bear a few opposite leaves which become divided higher up the stem.

Found in dry grassy places, grassy banks and slopes, roadsides, fields and pastures throughout Europe.

The similar Small Scabious has convex flower heads and the calyx of each flower has five bristly teeth (that of Field Scabious has 8 or 16 teeth) which remain as shiny black bristles on fruits. Devil's-bit Scabious grows in damp meadows and open woods; all flowers in its flower head are similar.

June–October.

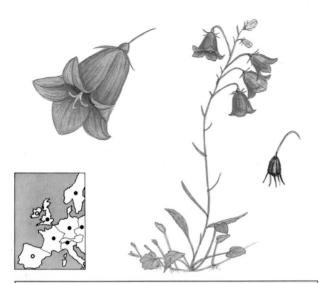

Blue bell-shaped flowers nod on long stalks on the delicate stems; the buds are erect. The flowers have linear sepals and five petal-lobes. The fruit is a rounded capsule with five sections, opening by pores at the base to release the seeds.

A delicate little perennial plant, with a clump of heart-shaped basal leaves. From this grow several erect, slender wiry stems with alternately arranged, dark green, linear leaves.

Found in dry grassland, on heaths and pastures on poor soils, also on dunes and in open woodland. In suitable habitats throughout Europe.

Bats-in-the-Belfry is a large plant of woods and hedgerows; its spikes of open bell-shaped flowers terminate clumps of leafy upright stems. Other bellflowers are grown in gardens. Bluebells are unrelated woodland plants with grass-like leaves and drooping, one-sided sprays of flowers in spring.

July–October.

Large flowers are lilac or rose-purple with darker veins; borne in clusters in upper leaf axils. Five petals are notched and widely separated from each other. Fruits are distinctive, like bristly segmented cheeses enclosed in a persistent calyx.

An annual or perennial plant with a stout, branched, hairy stem. Rounded lobed leaves are borne on long stalks in a basal rosette and arranged spirally on the stem. There is a leafy stipule at the base of each leaf stalk.

Found on roadsides and in waste places throughout Europe.

Dwarf Mallow is a sprawling annual plant, growing to 60cm:24in high, with kidney-shaped leaves; its flowers are whitish with lilac veins. Musk Mallow has erect stems with kidney-shaped basal leaves and divided upper leaves; it has solitary, large rose-pink flowers in the axils of the upper leaves.

May–September.

Flower head composed of a bristly, rounded "base" supporting a dense cluster of mauve to red-purple, tubular florets; heads solitary or borne in clusters at the top of the stem. Seeds have feathery hairs.

Spiny annual, biennial or perennial plants with erect stems and spirally arranged, deeply toothed or divided, spine-tipped leaves. Some species have spiny stems, in others the stems are spineless.

Found in waste places, cultivated ground and gardens, on roadsides, in fields and pastures throughout Europe.

Creeping (1) and Spear Thistles are weeds. Marsh Thistle has narrow continuous wings on its stems. Melancholy Thistle grows in grassland and woods, it has unwinged stems, flat spiny-edged leaves and few flower heads. Stemless Thistle has a flat rosette of spiny leaves; it grows on chalk and limestone.

July–October.

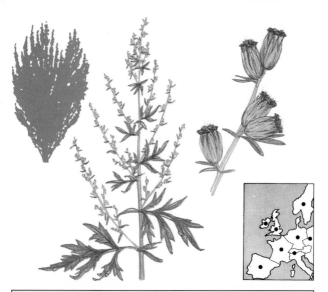

Numerous, tiny, erect, red-brown flower heads are borne in long, straight, leafy sprays terminating the branches of the stems. The bracts which cup the flower heads have dense spider-web hairs and papery margins.

A perennial, aromatic plant forming a clump of branched, erect stems. Stems are tough, grooved, angled, reddish and shortly hairy with many spirally arranged, dissected leaves. Leaves are dark green above, white with cottony hairs beneath.

Found on roadsides, in waste places and hedgerows throughout Europe.

Wormwood has whitish leaves and drooping, yellowish, almost spherical flower heads. It grows in cultivated ground and waste places. Sea Wormwood is a sprawling plant with woolly leaves and red-brown flower heads. It grows on sea walls and dry salt marshes, and in salt rich areas in inland Europe.

July–September.

95

Single flowers grow on long flower stalks in the leaf axils, opening only in sun. Petals five, bright red, joined at the base and falling as one unit. Fruits are rounded capsules cupped by sepals.

A small hairless annual weed with many branched, prostrate stems, often rooting at the nodes and forming a small spreading mat. Leaves opposite, small, ovate and stalkless.

Found on cultivated ground, on and beside paths and tracks, on roadsides and in waste land, and on dunes. Throughout Europe.

Scarlet Pimpernel, with its solitary bright red flowers, is not likely to be confused with other weeds. Bog Pimpernel has pale pink flowers and grows in wet grassland and bogs. Yellow Pimpernel and the larger Creeping Jenny have yellow flowers and grow in shady damp places.

June–August.

Flowers solitary, red, borne on long, bristly stalks in upper leaf axils. Buds drooping, with four bristly sepals. Fruits are egg-shaped capsules with a ring of holes beneath the cap. They act as peppershakers, scattering seeds in the wind.

An annual plant with a rosette of divided, long-stalked leaves and a clump of erect, leafy stems. The stems bear divided leaves and flowers; the whole plant is clothed with stiff hairs and full of white sap.

A weed of arable land and corn fields, now mostly confined to roadsides and waste places. Found throughout Europe.

The similar Long-headed Poppy is as common as Field Poppy in northern Europe; it has an elongated seed capsule. Prickly Long-headed Poppy is more common in southern areas, becoming rare in the north. The purple-flowered Opium Poppy is cultivated throughout Europe and often grows wild.

June–August.

97

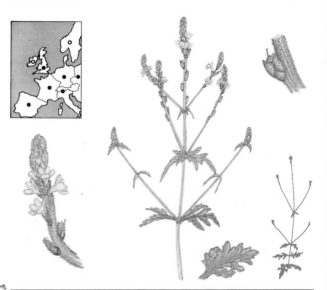

Flowers borne in stiff branching spikes which lengthen as the fruits ripen. Flowers small, pale lilac, the petals forming a tube with five spreading petal-lobes, the two upper lobes smallest. Fruit of four red-brown nutlets, enclosed in calyx.

A perennial plant with several stiff, erect, rather rough stems, branched like a candlestick and with terminal flower spikes. Lower parts of stem bear opposite pairs of large, rough, deeply toothed, often lobed, dull green leaves.

Found in waste places, on roadsides and besides tracks and paths, especially on chalk. Scattered throughout much of Europe.

Procumbent Vervain, from southern Europe, has weak stems which lie on the ground, divided leaves and small, pale lilac flowers.

July–September.

Numerous pink-purple flowers are borne in branching clusters terminating the stems. Each has five glandular-hairy sepals and five petals. Distinctive fruits are like five-part beaks which split into spoon-shaped sections, each with one seed.

A small branching, annual or biennial plant with a sprawling clump of strong, thin, hairy stems and palmately dissected leaves. The leaves are deep green, turning red in the sun or late in the year. The plant has a disagreeable odour.

Found in hedgerows and banks, amongst rocks and at the bases of walls, in woods and as a garden weed. Throughout Europe.

Cut-leaved Cranesbill is a small sprawling weed with dissected leaves; it has small pink flowers. Small-flowered Cranesbill is similar. Other cranesbills have palmately lobed leaves, like Dove's-foot Cranesbill, Round-leaved Cranesbill and the larger blue-flowered Meadow Cranesbill.

May–September.

99

LESSER BURDOCK
60–130cm:24–52in

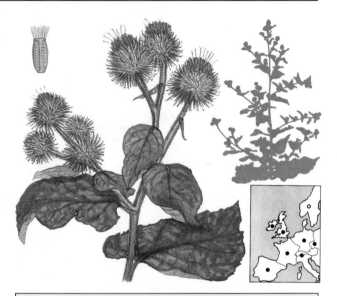

Red-purple flower heads are numerous, borne on long stalks in clusters terminating the branches of the stems. They are cupped in hooked bracts, which persist in fruit to form burrs. These get caught on animals and are dispersed whole.

A large biennial plant with a rosette of long-stalked pointed, narrowly heart-shaped leaves, up to 30cm:12in long, in the first year. Erect flower stems of second year are reddish, grooved and woolly with spirally arranged, heart-shaped leaves.

Found in waste places, beside tracks and on roadsides, in open woods and on woodland edges, in hedgerows. Throughout Europe.

Great Burdock is a bigger, less common plant with rounded heart-shaped leaves which lack the pointed tips of those of Lesser Burdock. Woolly Burdock has a network of cobwebby hairs covering the bracts of the flower heads; it is absent from Britain and Iberia.

July–September.

Rosy purple flowers have four petals; borne in large terminal flowering spikes. The flower buds droop before opening. Seed capsules are erect and up to 8cm:3¼in long; they split longitudinally to release many feathery seeds.

A perennial plant with widely spreading roots, from which grow large numbers of tall erect leafy stems. Leaves are long and narrow, dark green and angled upwards, alternate or spirally arranged on the stems.

Often forms wide colonies in woodland clearings and on disturbed ground, especially after fire; also in waste places, gardens, hedgerows and rocky places. Throughout Europe.

In other willow-herbs the flowers grow horizontally instead of pointing upwards. Several small willow-herbs, with small pale pink flowers, grow as weeds in gardens and waste places. Great Hairy Willow-herb is a tall leafy plant of streambanks and ditches; it has large rose-pink flowers with creamy stigmas.

July–September.

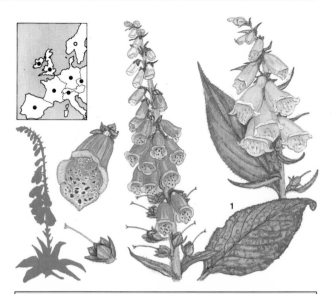

Flowers large and conspicuous, like hanging, curved, purple bells with dark spots inside. They are borne in a long one-sided spike terminating the single, upright stem. Fruits are black, egg-shaped capsules.

A softly hairy, biennial plant with a rosette of large, lance-shaped, rough-textured leaves in the first year and the erect flowering stalk in the second. This has similar but smaller leaves with winged leaf-stalks. **Poisonous**, contains digitalin.

Found in woodland clearings, especially in burnt areas and on light acid soils, heaths and mountains. Western Europe from Norway, through Britain and France to Spain.

Large Yellow Foxglove (1), from much of Europe (absent in north and Britain), has pale yellow flowers with brown veins inside, and lance-shaped, hairless, shiny leaves. Rusty Foxglove, from southeast Europe, has globular, red-yellow flowers with a long lower lip, and long lance-shaped, hairless leaves.

June–September.

COMMON CENTAURY
5–50cm:2–20in

Flowers pink and tubular with five spreading petal-lobes above a tubular calyx; borne in terminal clusters on upright flower stalks. Five stamens are inserted at the top of the petal-tube. Fruits are capsules projecting above persistent calyx.

A hairless, annual plant with a basal rosette of elliptical, pointed leaves and usually a single branched, upright flowering stalk. This bears a few opposite pairs of leaves. The leaves have three to seven prominent veins.

Found in dry grassland, woodland edges and on dunes. Throughout Europe.

There are several other species of Centaury growing in grassland and near the sea. Slender Centaury, a maritime species, has no basal rosette of leaves. Felwort has upright, tubular, purplish flowers with a fringe of white hairs in the throat; it grows on limestone grassland and dunes.

June–October.

Solitary flower heads, 2–4cm:¾–1½in in diameter, terminate the stem branches; they have many similar, red-purple florets, cupped in a ball of dark brown bracts which have spiky teeth. Seeds are pale brown with a ring of short hairs around the top.

A perennial plant which forms a clump of tough, grooved, roughly hairy stems, branched near the top. The basal leaves are entire with sinuately toothed edges and long stalks; upper leaves are entire without stalks. All leaves are hairy.

Found in grassland, on roadsides, banks and cliffs. Throughout Europe.

Greater Knapweed is a less common plant found in similar habitats; its flower heads have a ring of large spreading florets around the edge. Saw-wort has dark brown bracts cupping the flower heads but these lack spiky margins; it grows in woods and grassland on chalk and limestone.

July–September.

EARLY PURPLE ORCHID
15–60cm:6–24in

Flowers borne in a broad open spike; usually crimson-purple with darker spots but varying to light pink. They are hooded and spurred with a horizontal or upwardly pointed spur and a three-lobed, spotted lower lip.

These plants take several years to reach flowering stage, then die. Young plants have one or two leaves; mature plants have a rosette of lance-shaped leaves which sheath the base of the erect flowering stem. Leaves have round purple-black spots.

Found in woods and copses, downs and pastures, sea and mountain cliffs, most often on neutral or calcareous soils. Throughout most of Europe.

Green-winged Orchid grows on pastures and downs, usually on calcareous soils; it has unspotted leaves and distinct green veins on the flowers. Spotted Orchids have a downwardly pointing spur on their pink flowers. Meadow Orchids have unspotted leaves and downwardly pointing flower spurs.

April–July.

WILD THYME
5cm : 2in

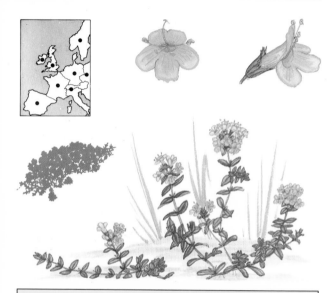

Flowers in heads, borne on rows of erect flower stems. They are pink-purple in colour, tubular with four petal-lobes. Calyx purple-tipped with two lips; three sepals in upper lip, two in lower lip. Nutlets dark brown and smooth, in fours.

A mat-forming, perennial plant with many creeping branches which spread in all directions, rooting as they grow. They have many small, elliptical leaves which grow horizontally. The four-angled flower stems have hairs on two opposite sides.

Found on dry grassland, downs and heaths, amongst rocks, on screes and dunes. Throughout Europe.

Large Wild Thyme has erect, four-angled flower stems up to 25cm:10in tall; hairs grow on the angles of the stems. The flowers of this plant are pink-purple, borne in elongated heads. Cultivated Thyme is a small branched shrub with pink flowers and greyish leaves; it grows in dry places in southern Europe.

May–August.

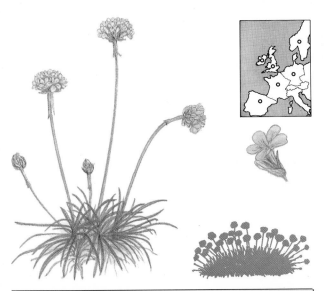

Rose-pink flowers have five petals joined at the base and a tubular calyx; borne in dense, hemispherical heads on long stalks. Bracts sheath each flower, the outer ones papery, inner ones green. Fruits form in withered persistent flowers.

A tufted cushion or carpet-forming, perennial plant. It has a woody, branched base from which grow many rosettes of long, narrow, dark green, grass-like leaves. Each rosette may produce one flower head.

Usually a maritime plant growing on coastal rocks and cliffs, in salt-marshes and coastal pastures but also found on mountains. Western and northern Europe.

Alpine Thrift grows in the high Alps, Pyrenees and Carpathians. It is similar to Thrift but smaller, with broader leaves and bright pink flowers in spherical heads.

May–August.

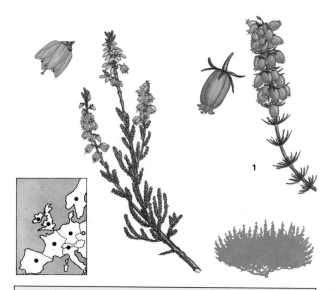

Flowers borne in loose spikes, growing in the axils of the upper leaves. Each flower has four pale purple sepals alternating with four similar petals and is cupped in small green bracts. Fruits are round capsules.

A branched, evergreen shrub, with numerous woody stems, clothed with very small, dark green leaves. The leaves are linear in shape, stalkless and arranged in four overlapping rows; each has two small projections at the base.

Found on heaths and moors, and in open woods, on acid soils throughout Europe; often dominant, making the landscape dull green for much of the year and transforming it in flower.

Bell-heather (1) has larger leaves arranged in whorls of three and much larger, distinctly bell-shaped, crimson-purple flowers. Cross-leaved Heath grows in wet heaths and bogs; it has whorls of four leaves (which resemble a cross) and terminal clusters of bell-shaped pink flowers.

July–October.

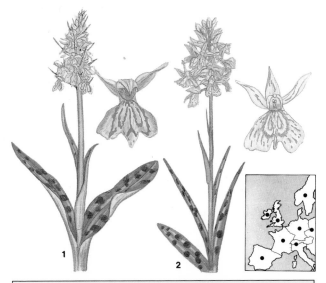

Flowers hooded, with a three-lobed, spotted lower lip, and a downwardly pointing spur; colour varies from pink to white with pink markings. Flower spike appears pyramidal when early flowers open, it broadens at the top as upper flowers open.

A perennial plant with an erect flower stem and a small clump of broadly elliptical or lance-shaped leaves, the lowermost largest, upper ones small and clasping the stem. Leaves are keeled, with edges folded upwards and dark circular spots.

Found in damp meadows, fens and bogs, on grassy banks, on moors and heaths. Throughout Europe.

Two species of Spotted Orchid occur in Europe, **Common Spotted Orchid** (1) and **Heath Spotted Orchid** (2). The former grows on basic soils in Western Europe and Britain, the latter on acid soils throughout Europe. Common Spotted has pink flowers while Heath Spotted has white, pink-spotted flowers.

June–August.

109

Flowers have four pink or lilac, veined petals; they are borne in conspicuous terminal, lengthening clusters. Fruits are long thin pods held at an angle to the stem. They open suddenly, the two valves coiling from the base and flinging out seeds.

A small, almost hairless, perennial plant. It has a basal rosette of long-stalked, compound leaves with oval, toothed leaflets, and several erect leafy stems. Stem leaves have lance-shaped leaflets, arranged alternately.

Found beside streams, in damp meadows and grassland, throughout Europe.

The similar Large Bittercress has white flowers; it grows on streambanks and near springs, especially on peaty soil. Wood Bittercress, also with white flowers, grows in shady places. Watercress is a succulent plant with dark green leaves and white flowers; it grows in streams and other wet places.

April–June.

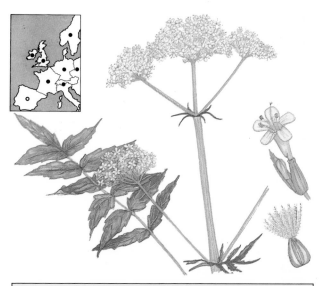

Flowers pale pink, tubular, slightly swollen at the base, with five petal-lobes; borne in three-forked, dense terminal heads. Flowers have a small, inrolled calyx at the base. As fruits enlarge, the calyx unrolls and forms a feathery parachute.

A perennial, almost hairless plant which forms a clump of erect leafy stems. The leaves are opposite, pinnate with lance-shaped, toothed leaflets; lowermost are long-stalked with grooved leaf bases, upper ones almost stalkless.

Found in rough grassland, meadows and woodland, usually in wet or damp places, also beside water. Throughout Europe.

The smaller Marsh Valerian has creeping, rooting stems with simple, rounded lower leaves and divided upper leaves; pinkish male and female flowers are borne on separate plants. Red Valerian forms large leafy clumps on old walls and dry banks and cliffs. It has open, head-like clusters of red flowers.

May–August.

111

Flowers lilac, small and tubular with four petal-lobes and four protruding stamens; arranged in a dense terminal spike and in several whorls in the uppermost leaf axils. Fruits are smooth, egg-shaped nutlets in fours, in persistent calyx.

A perennial plant with many erect, four-angled, often branched stems, frequently red-coloured when exposed to sun. Stems bear many opposite, long-stalked, ovate, often hairy leaves. The whole plant has a strong distinctive scent of mint.

Found in marshes and fens, beside rivers and ponds and in other wet places throughout Europe.

Spearmint has its own characteristic scent; it has pointed, lance-shaped, more or less hairless leaves, and a terminal spike of lilac flowers, separated into several whorls. Corn Mint has whorls of lilac flowers in the leaf axils; its scent is acrid. Both grow in damp places.

July–October.

Flowers pink, borne in tight spikes, often with a single leaf at the base of the spike. The pink colour of the flowers comes from the sepals, for petals are absent. Brown, shining fruits are borne in similar spikes.

A spreading annual plant, with several smooth reddish stems. Swellings above the nodes give the stems an angular appearance. Leaves alternate, lance-shaped, often blotched with black and with fringed leaf sheaths at their bases.

Found in waste places, beside paths and tracks, especially on damp ground; also beside water and in ditches. Throughout Europe.

Knotgrass (1) is a common weed with small bluish leaves, silvery leaf sheaths and tiny white or pinkish flowers. Pale Persicaria has green stems, leaf sheaths without fringes and white or green flowers. Water-pepper has nodding spikes of pink-green flowers; it grows in wet places and shallow water.

June–October.

Flowers large and highly distinctive; purple and shaped like a helmet. They are borne on long stalks in open clusters in the axils of the upper leaves. The long ripe fruiting capsules burst open when touched, showering out a fusillade of seeds.

A robust, leafy, annual plant with stout reddish stems. It is hairless. The large, toothed, lance-shaped leaves are borne in opposite pairs or in whorls of three.

Introduced from the Himalayas. Naturalized and spreading rapidly on river and stream banks, on the sides of ditches and canals and in waste places throughout much of Europe.

There is no other plant quite like this one. The related Touch-me-not and Orange Balsam are smaller plants, also annuals with similar shaped flowers, but the first has yellow flowers and the second orange ones.

July–October.

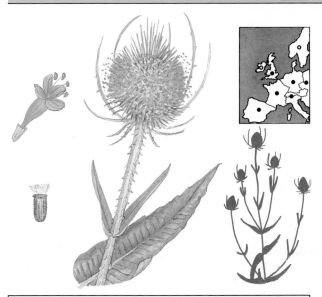

Rose-purple flowers are borne in distinctive, terminal prickly flower heads, the earliest blooming in a ring around the centre of the head and later flowers spreading up and down. The flower heads remain to form prickly fruits, the teasels.

A large biennial plant with a clump of prickly leaves in the first year. In the second year, erect, hollow, prickly stems bear long, lance-shaped, opposite leaves; the leaf bases are fused across the stem to form cups where water collects.

Found on roadsides, especially on the banks of ditches and in wet places, also in west grassland and woods, and beside streams. Scattered throughout Europe.

Small Teasel is a much less common plant of damp woods and hedgebanks. It grows up to 100cm:40in tall and has spherical flower heads with whitish flowers. Teasels are easy to distinguish from **Burdocks** or **Thistles** for these plants have flowers on top of a prickly receptacle and hairy seeds afterwards.

Flowers: July–Aug. Fruits: Sept.–Oct. and often persist.

115

OTHER COMMON SPECIES

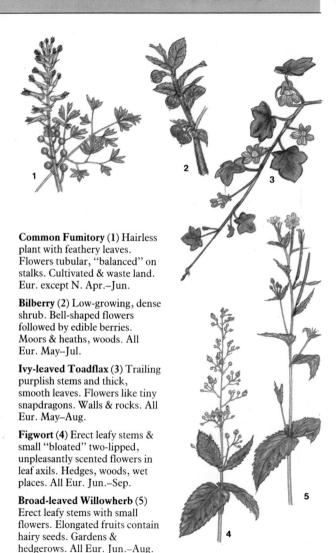

Common Fumitory (1) Hairless plant with feathery leaves. Flowers tubular, "balanced" on stalks. Cultivated & waste land. Eur. except N. Apr.–Jun.

Bilberry (2) Low-growing, dense shrub. Bell-shaped flowers followed by edible berries. Moors & heaths, woods. All Eur. May–Jul.

Ivy-leaved Toadflax (3) Trailing purplish stems and thick, smooth leaves. Flowers like tiny snapdragons. Walls & rocks. All Eur. May–Aug.

Figwort (4) Erect leafy stems & small "bloated" two-lipped, unpleasantly scented flowers in leaf axils. Hedges, woods, wet places. All Eur. Jun.–Sep.

Broad-leaved Willowherb (5) Erect leafy stems with small flowers. Elongated fruits contain hairy seeds. Gardens & hedgerows. All Eur. Jun.–Aug.

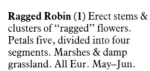

Ragged Robin (1) Erect stems & clusters of "ragged" flowers. Petals five, divided into four segments. Marshes & damp grassland. All Eur. May–Jun.

Hedge Woundwort (2) Erect leafy stems bear whorls of two-lipped flowers in upper leaf axils. Woods & hedgerows. All Eur. Jun.–Sep.

Common Hempnettle (3) Erect leafy, hairy stems bear whorls of two-lipped flowers in leaf axils. Arable land, woods, wet heaths. All Eur. Jun.–Oct.

Purple Loosestrife (4) Tall leafy stems bear flowers in whorls of six. Each flower has six petals. Watersides & marshes. All Eur. Jun.–Sep.

Hemp Agrimony (5) Tall leafy stems with flat-topped flower heads. Seeds have white parachutes. Stream banks, marshes, wet woods. All Eur. Jul.–Aug.

Bindweeds have funnel-shaped flowers growing in the leaf axils. The white flowers of Greater Bindweed grow singly and are 5cm:2in long; those of Field Bindweed are pink, about 2½cm:1in long and may grow in ones or pairs.

These two troublesome weeds are perennial twining vines with deep spreading roots which can penetrate a metre:40in into the ground. Their smooth arrow-shaped leaves are larger in Greater Bindweed (up to 15cm:6in long).

Found in waste places, cultivated land and gardens, roadsides and beside railways, twining in fences and hedges, in woods and near the sea. Throughout Europe but less common in north.

Sea Bindweed grows on shingle banks and dunes near the sea; it has creeping stems, kidney-shaped leaves and pink flowers. Mallow-leaved Bindweed, from the Mediterranean, grows in cultivated land and on waysides. It is a twining plant with lobed upper leaves; its pink flowers have a dark pink throat.

May–October.

118

Flowers distinctive in shape, two-lipped; the upper lip spurred, the lower lip boat-shaped. They are borne in small sprays in the axils of the uppermost leaves, "balanced on their stalks". Fruits are cylindrical capsules.

Smooth, brittle and hairless plants, rather bluish in colour and forming small perennial clumps of fern-like, deeply dissected leaves.

Yellow Corydalis (1) grows on old walls or amongst rocks in western Europe. **Purple Corydalis** (2) is found in spring in vineyards, woods and hedgerows in much of Europe.

There are several other Corydalis species in Europe. Climbing Corydalis is an annual climbing plant which has cream flowers in summer; it grows in woods and amongst rocks. Fumitories are small related weeds of arable land and waste places, with similar flowers in shades of pink and purple.

April–September.

1

2

Flowers borne in tight heads on long stalks in leaf axils. They are pea-like, purplish red or white, often tinged with pink and with abundant nectar at the base of the tube. Fruits are small pods enclosed in dead persistent flowers.

Perennial plants, with many thin creeping stems rooting at the nodes. Leaves with three leaflets, in some species with a distinctive pale crescentic band around the base of each leaflet.

Common plants of grassy places, tracks and roadsides, on downs and heaths, in meadows, lawns and gardens. Throughout Europe.

There are many Clovers, of which most common are **White Clover** (1) and **Red Clover** (2), both with similar crescentic marks on their leaves. Alsike Clover has plain unmarked leaflets and pinkish-white flowers. Zig-zag Clover has long leaflets, often with a faint whitish spot, and red-purple flowers.

May–September.

Flowers vary in colour, from white to yellow-white, pink or purple. They are tubular and borne in coiled, one-sided clusters on long stalks in the leaf axils. Fruit consists of four shining black nutlets, cupped in persistent calyx.

A perennial plant which forms a large clump of leafy stems. Leaves are large, rough and hairy, broadly lance-shaped. The upper leaves are stalkless and their broad bases run down the stem to the leaf below; the lower leaves have winged stalks.

Found in damp places, meadows, watersides and ditches. Most of Europe but more common in the south than in the north.

Blue Comfrey grows in hedges and on roadsides. It has blue or purple flowers; the narrow leaf bases on its upper leaves run down the stem from one leaf to the leaf below. Tuberous Comfrey grows in damp meadows and beside water, more commonly in northern Europe than in the south; it has yellow flowers.

May–June.

121

Index and Checklist

All species in roman type are illustrated.
Keep a record of your sightings by ticking the boxes.